A game book for kids ages 6-12

SILLY BEAR

Published by On the Hop Books Ltd

This game book is a word game book only and is not suitable for any other use than conversation. No scenarios should be enacted at any time by any person and children should be supervised at all times by a responsible adult.

This book is printed in the country of purchase.

ISBN: 978-1-9162936-3-2

How to Play

This book can be read just for fun...

OR: Play it with others

With two or more people, one person can choose the question to ask the next person.
All of the questions offer two pretend scenarios where a choice must be made.
The person being asked the question has to give an answer, they cannot say both or neither.
The person who just answered a question then gets to choose and ask the next question to the next person.
The idea is to have fun and open up a conversation with friends and family.

OR: Options for points

Here's some ideas for how to play the game so that people win points. You may need a pencil and paper for these. Play first to 3,5 or 10 points.

1. Trying not to laugh. If the person answering a question doesn't laugh during their turn answering, they get one point. Everyone else can choose any strategy to make the person answering laugh during their turn.

2. A no hesitation challenge. The person answering cannot hesitate or say 'erm / er / I don't know / neither' (or other stalling type noises or words) whilst answering. If they succeed, the person answering wins 1 point.

3. A Don't Blink Challenge. This can be played two ways. Either the person answering has to answer without blinking and if they succeed, they win 1 point. OR: play it where both the person asking and the person answering must not blink. Whoever blinks first loses and the other person wins 1 point.

WHICH WOULD YOU CHOOSE?

Would you prefer to have super long distance eye sight

have super long distance hearing?

Would you prefer to have ears made of waffles

have fingers made of cake?

Would you prefer to live in a cave

live in an igloo?

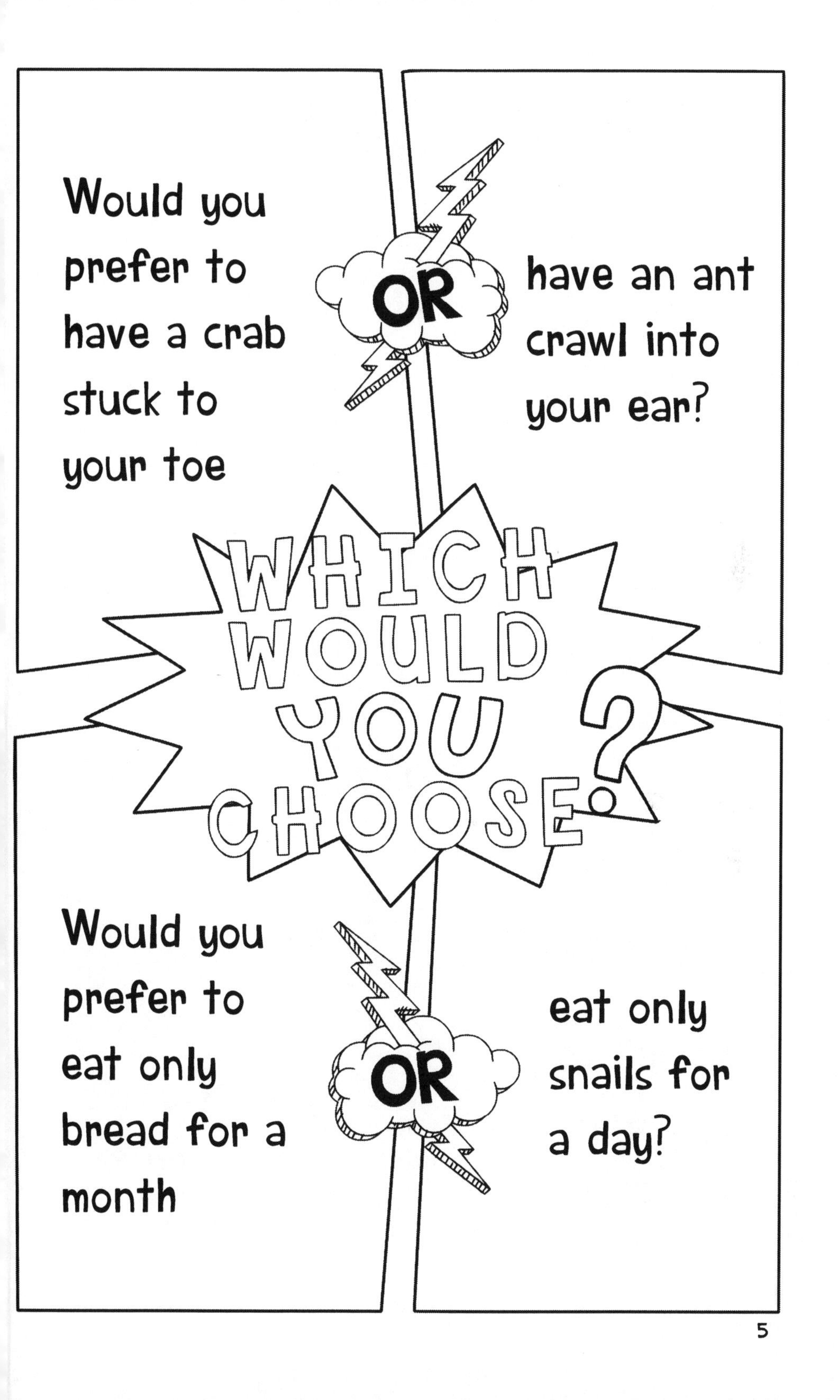
Would you prefer to have a crab stuck to your toe
OR
have an ant crawl into your ear?
WHICH WOULD YOU CHOOSE?
Would you prefer to eat only bread for a month
OR
eat only snails for a day?

WHICH WOULD YOU CHOOSE?

Would you prefer to be a film star

be a film maker?

Would you prefer to have a giant moustache

have a long curly beard?

Would you prefer to live without toilet paper

live without an oven to cook in?

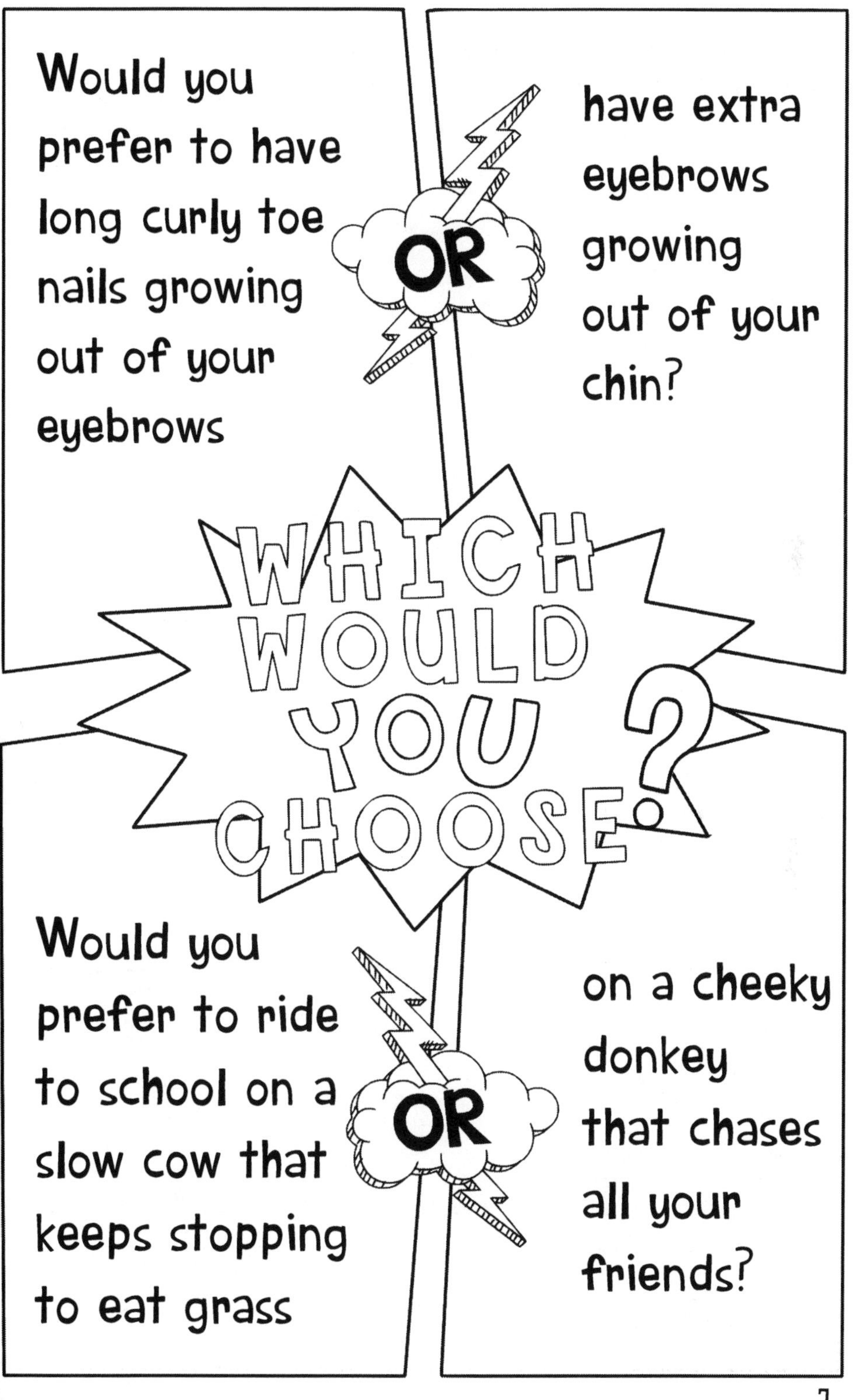
Would you prefer to have long curly toe nails growing out of your eyebrows
OR
have extra eyebrows growing out of your chin?
WHICH WOULD YOU CHOOSE?
Would you prefer to ride to school on a slow cow that keeps stopping to eat grass
OR
on a cheeky donkey that chases all your friends?

WHICH WOULD YOU CHOOSE?

Would you prefer to have music to listen to

OR

books to read?

Would you prefer to have no more television

no more modern medicine?

Would you prefer to go running in the rain

bask in the sun by a pool?

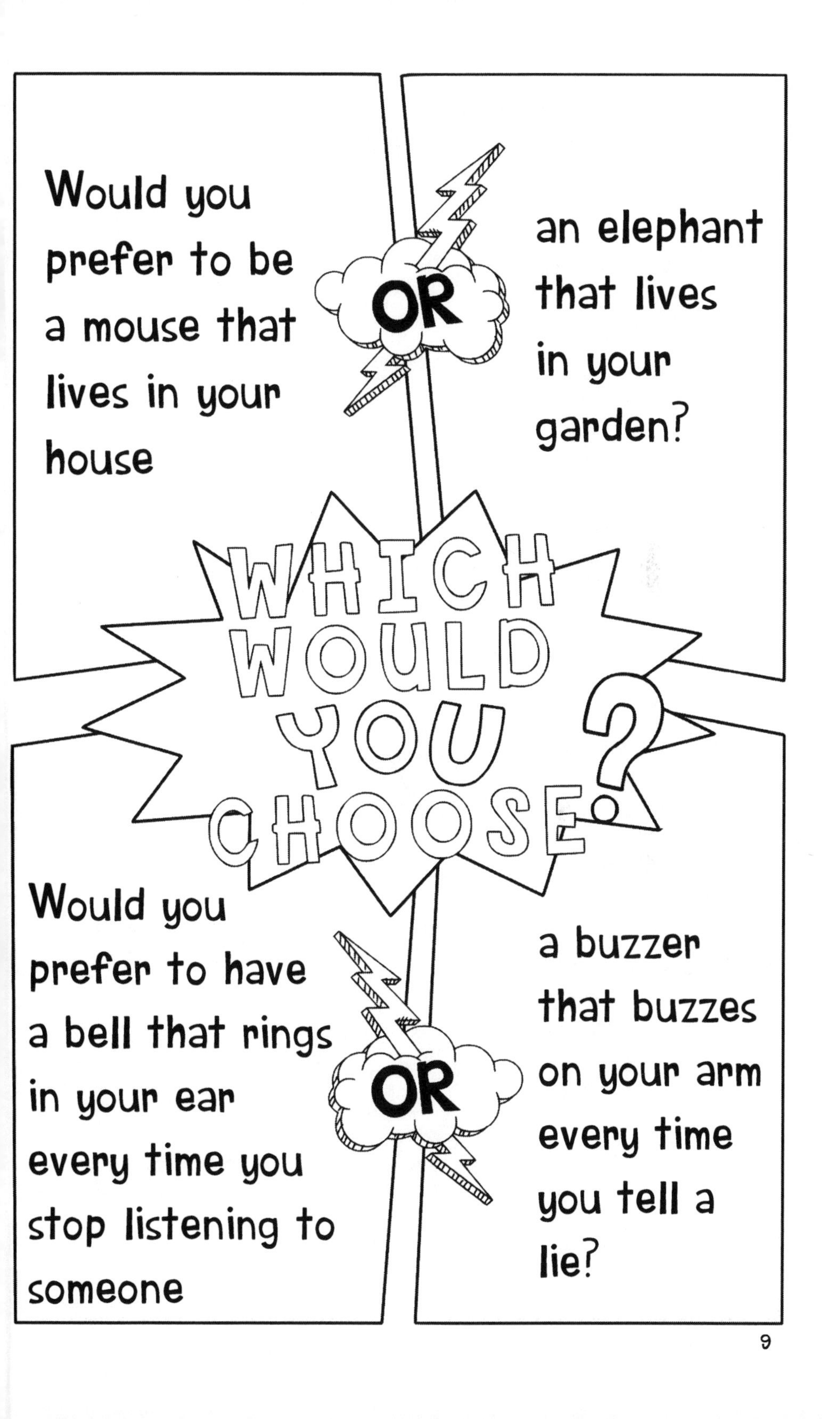
Would you prefer to be a mouse that lives in your house
OR
an elephant that lives in your garden?
WHICH WOULD YOU CHOOSE?
Would you prefer to have a bell that rings in your ear every time you stop listening to someone
OR
a buzzer that buzzes on your arm every time you tell a lie?

WHICH WOULD YOU CHOOSE?

Would you prefer to go to school wearing clothes covered in barbecue sauce

OR

clothes covered in vinegar?

Would you prefer to have a puppy as a pet

a kitten?

Would you prefer to be a ninja

a spy?

Would you prefer to travel through space with karaoke obssessed aliens who won't stop singing
OR
have some quiet aliens live at your house for a year?
WHICH WOULD YOU CHOOSE?
Would you prefer to have a rainbow shine light on your head all day
OR
have a rain cloud rain over your head for an hour every morning?

WHICH WOULD YOU CHOOSE?

Would you prefer to wear cobwebs in your hair

have bird nests for shoes?

Would you prefer to be a monkey

a lion?

Would you prefer to eat ice-cream

cake?

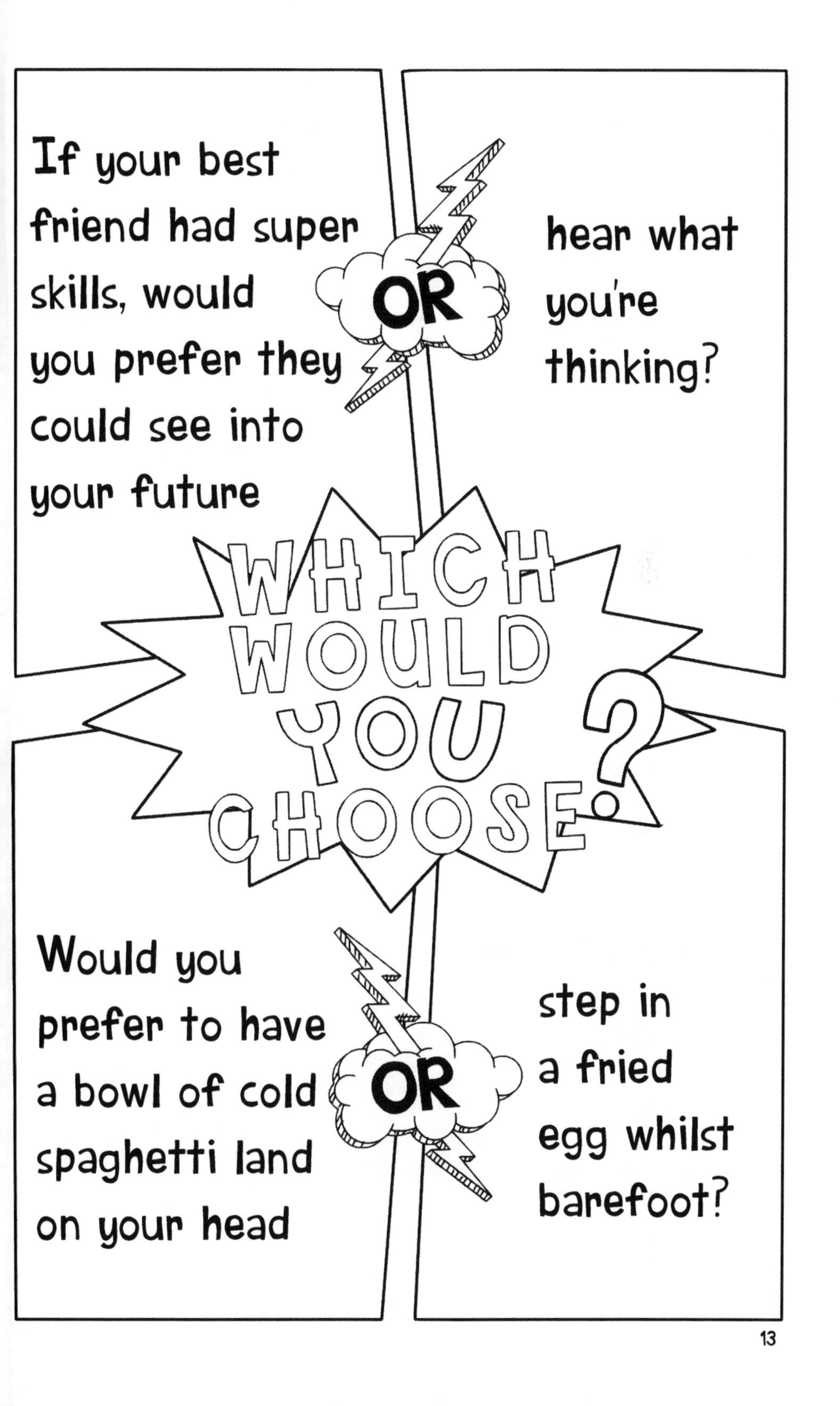
If your best friend had super skills, would you prefer they could see into your future
OR
hear what you're thinking?
WHICH WOULD YOU CHOOSE?
Would you prefer to have a bowl of cold spaghetti land on your head
OR
step in a fried egg whilst barefoot?

WHICH WOULD YOU CHOOSE?

Would you prefer to travel to the moon

travel to the opposite side of the planet?

Would you prefer to have a voice that sounds like a bark

a voice that sounds like a squeak?

Would you prefer that apples didn't exist

oranges didn't exist?

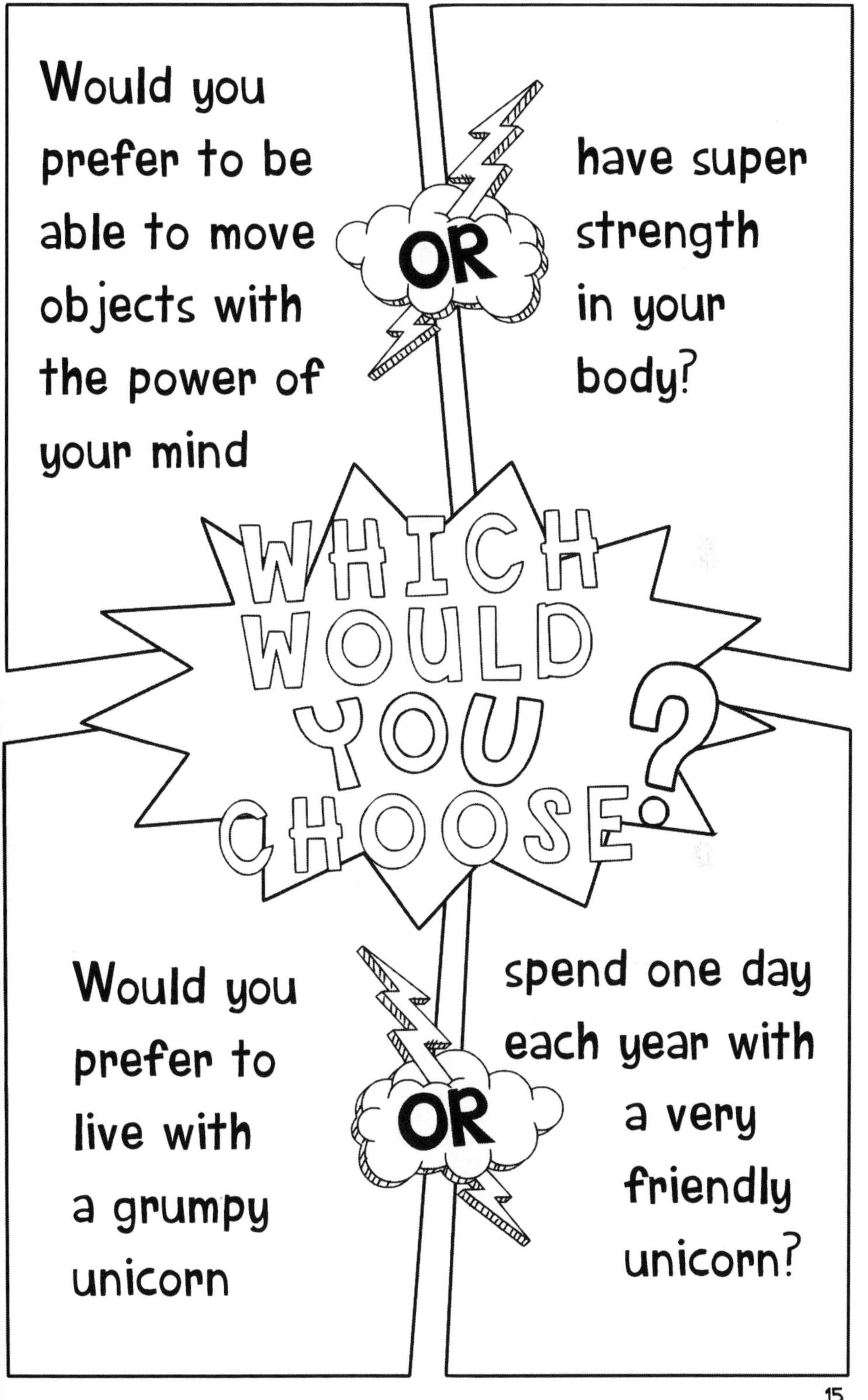
Would you prefer to be able to move objects with the power of your mind
OR
have super strength in your body?
WHICH WOULD YOU CHOOSE?
Would you prefer to live with a grumpy unicorn
OR
spend one day each year with a very friendly unicorn?

WHICH WOULD YOU CHOOSE?

Would you prefer to be able to fly

teleport as a super power?

Would you prefer to take a shower in glitter glue water

a bath in a liquid rainbow?

Would you prefer to not be able to taste chocolate

not be able to taste cheese?

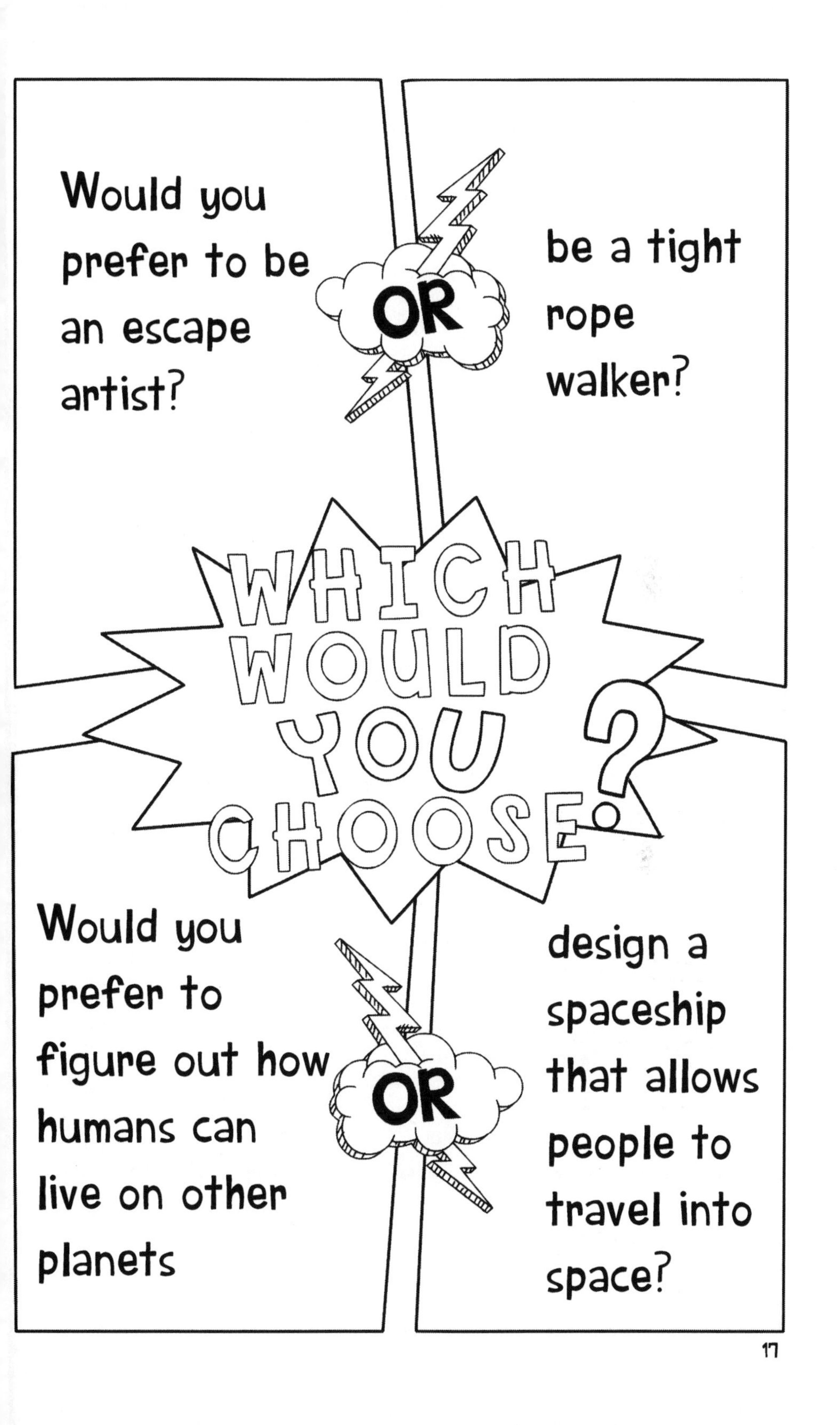
Would you prefer to be an escape artist?
OR
be a tight rope walker?
WHICH WOULD YOU CHOOSE?
Would you prefer to figure out how humans can live on other planets
OR
design a spaceship that allows people to travel into space?

WHICH WOULD YOU CHOOSE?

Would you prefer to have an itch all week on your nose

an itch all week on your bottom?

Would you prefer to be a pirate with one leg

a pirate with an eye patch?

Would you prefer to have a bed to sleep in

have a sofa to sit on?

Would you prefer to find that your favorite treat tasted like carrots for a whole month
OR
find it tasted like sour lemon for a whole month instead?
WHICH WOULD YOU CHOOSE?
Would you prefer to celebrate your birthday flying with dragons
OR
spend your birthday in space with aliens?

WHICH WOULD YOU CHOOSE?

Would you prefer to watch a movie with no treats to eat

OR

have treats to eat but no movie to watch?

Would you prefer to be a sports star

OR

a pop star?

Would you prefer to have lunch with a giraffe

OR

a sloth?

Would you prefer to eat a slice of cake that has cooked garlic in it
OR
eat a piece of chocolate that has raw onion in it?
WHICH WOULD YOU CHOOSE?
Would you prefer to live on the moon for 3 months
OR
live in Antarctica for 6 months?

WHICH WOULD YOU CHOOSE?

Would you prefer to eat roasted crickets

eat frogs' legs soup?

Would you prefer to be a fairy

be a giant?

Would you prefer that candy and sweets didn't exist

ice-cream didn't exist?

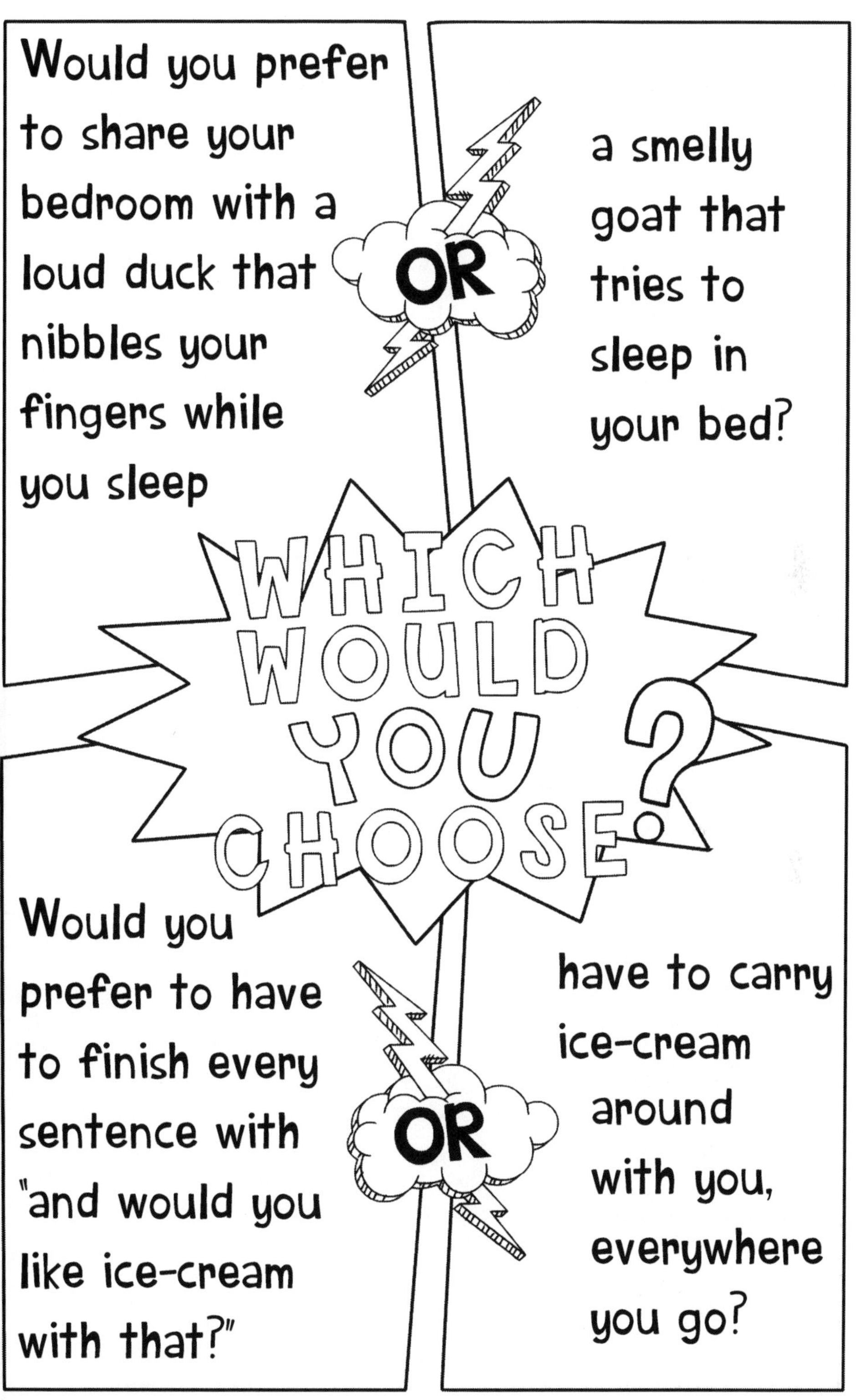
Would you prefer to share your bedroom with a loud duck that nibbles your fingers while you sleep
OR
a smelly goat that tries to sleep in your bed?
WHICH WOULD YOU CHOOSE?
Would you prefer to have to finish every sentence with "and would you like ice-cream with that?"
OR
have to carry ice-cream around with you, everywhere you go?

WHICH WOULD YOU CHOOSE?

Would you prefer to live by the beach

on a mountainside?

Would you prefer to wear your pants on your head

your shoes on your hands?

Would you prefer to own a bicycle

a trampoline?

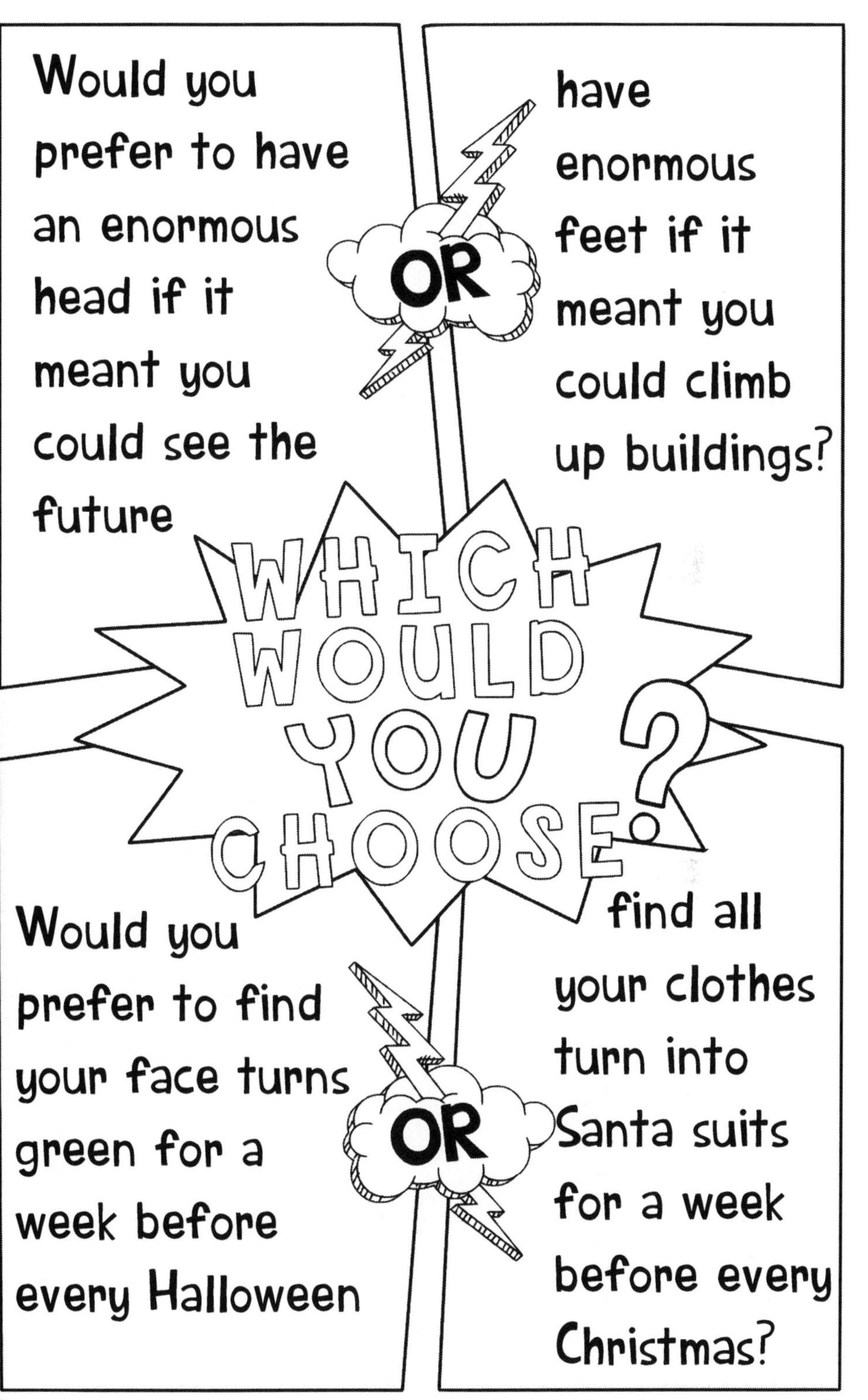
Would you prefer to have an enormous head if it meant you could see the future
OR
have enormous feet if it meant you could climb up buildings?
WHICH WOULD YOU CHOOSE?
Would you prefer to find your face turns green for a week before every Halloween
OR
find all your clothes turn into Santa suits for a week before every Christmas?

WHICH WOULD YOU CHOOSE?

Would you prefer to know morse code

sign language?

Would you prefer to wear a hat that sings Christmas songs non-stop

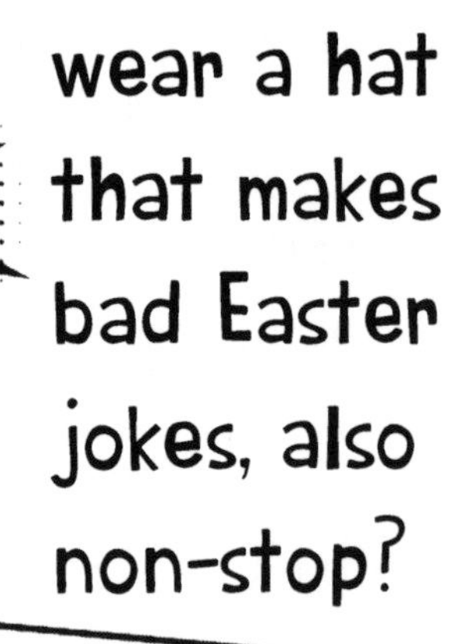

wear a hat that makes bad Easter jokes, also non-stop?

Would you prefer to be a doctor

a fireman / firewoman?

Would you prefer to get an extra day of holiday where you choose what to do?
OR
get an extra week of holiday where your family choose what to do?
WHICH WOULD YOU CHOOSE?
Would you prefer to wear a long black coat every day that makes you look like an angry wizard
OR
wear a disco outfit every day covered in bright rainbow patterns?

WHICH WOULD YOU CHOOSE?

Would you prefer to have cauliflower growing out of your armpits

OR

seaweed growing out of your bellybutton?

Would you prefer to be a famous inventor

a famous movie star?

Would you prefer to have 3 extra hours a day for yourself

3 extra hours a day to spend with your family?

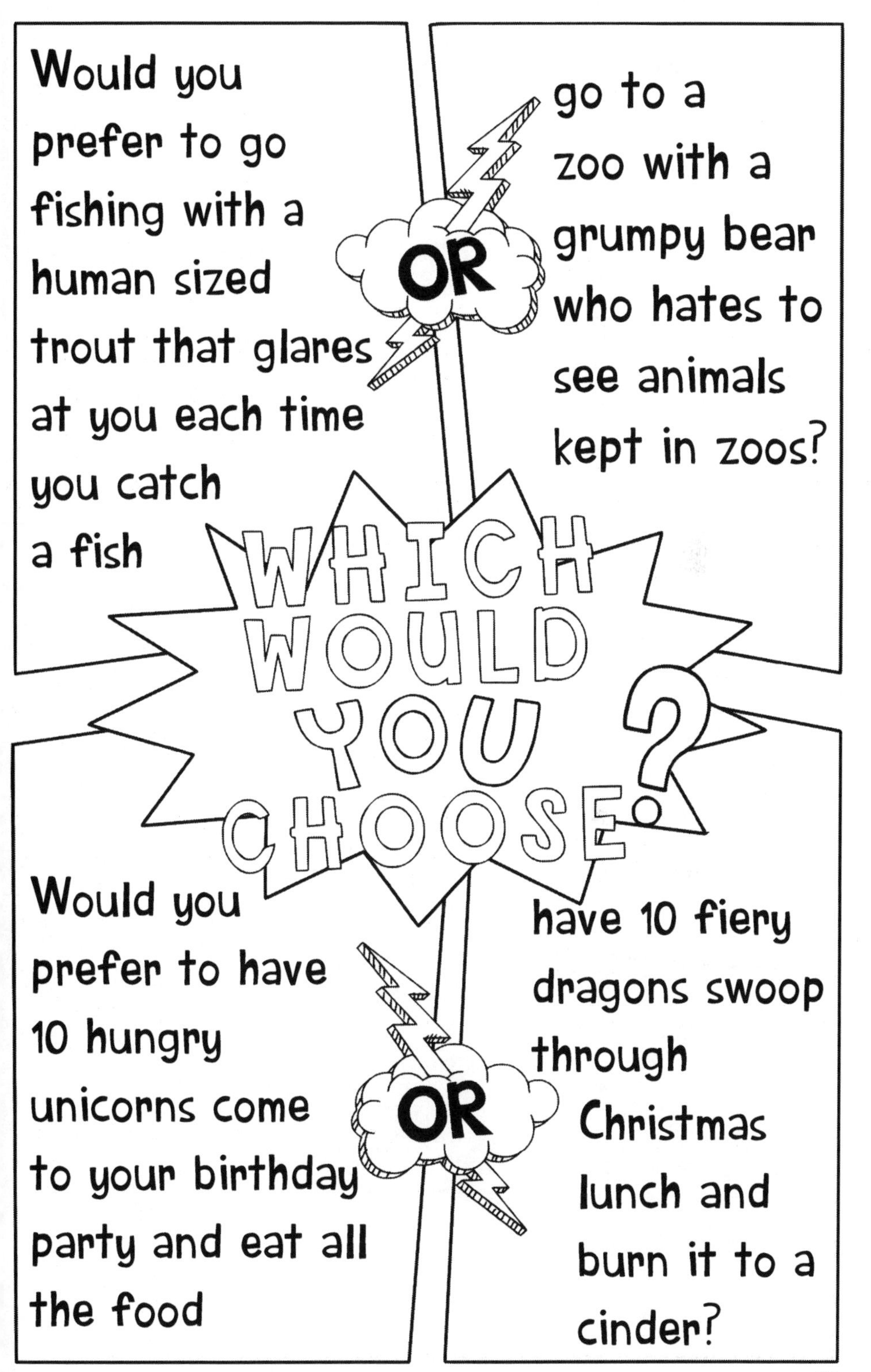
Would you prefer to go fishing with a human sized trout that glares at you each time you catch a fish
OR
go to a zoo with a grumpy bear who hates to see animals kept in zoos?
WHICH WOULD YOU CHOOSE?
Would you prefer to have 10 hungry unicorns come to your birthday party and eat all the food
OR
have 10 fiery dragons swoop through Christmas lunch and burn it to a cinder?

WHICH WOULD YOU CHOOSE?

Would you prefer to have to breakdance your way to school

hopscotch your way back?

Would you prefer to live in a house with lights

a house with a cooker, if you had to choose?

Would you prefer to have fox ears

cat whiskers?

Would you prefer to be a successful artist
OR
a successful author?
WHICH WOULD YOU CHOOSE?
Would you prefer to be a real life superhero, like a fireman, nurse or doctor
OR
be an actor playing a make believe superhero in a film?

WHICH WOULD YOU CHOOSE?

Would you prefer to have all your fingernails painted red for a year

OR

your hair dyed bright green for a month?

Would you prefer to be a strong man in a circus

OR

be part of the trapeze act?

Would you prefer to teleport to another planet with life on it

OR

teleport to another time in Planet Earth's history?

Would you prefer to eat ice-cream when it's freezing cold outside
OR
drink hot drinks during a heatwave?
WHICH WOULD YOU CHOOSE?
Would you prefer to have a pet parrot that repeats everything you say at the worst possible moment
OR
a pet dog that eats all your homework as soon as you finish it?

WHICH WOULD YOU CHOOSE?

Would you prefer to have feet that can turn into seal's flippers

OR

the agility of a cat?

Would you prefer to be able to travel back in time

forwards in time?

Would you prefer to be able to smell sweet popcorn all of the time

OR

smell fresh lemons all of the time?

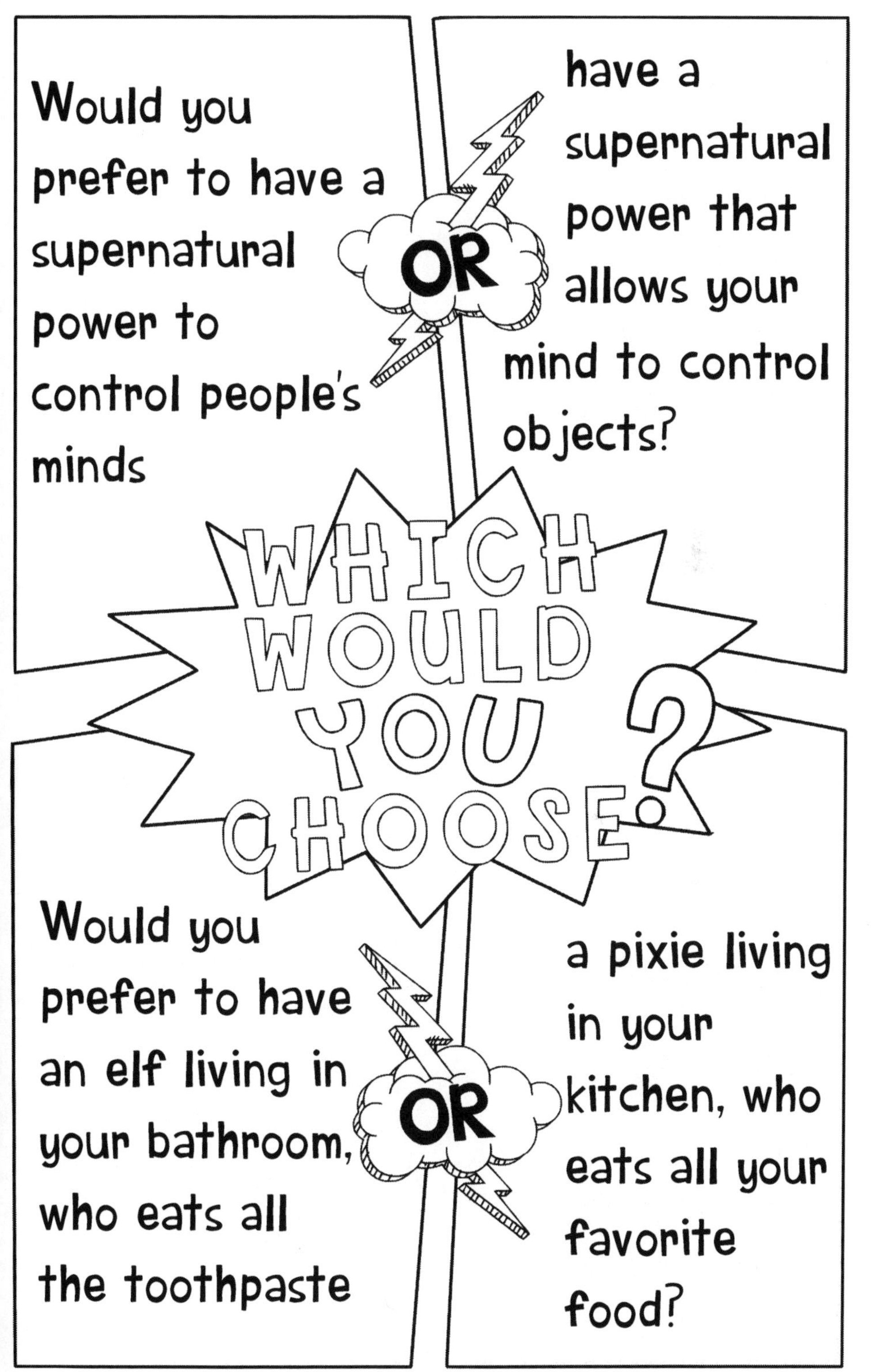

Would you prefer to have a supernatural power to control people's minds
OR
have a supernatural power that allows your mind to control objects?
WHICH WOULD YOU CHOOSE?
Would you prefer to have an elf living in your bathroom, who eats all the toothpaste
OR
a pixie living in your kitchen, who eats all your favorite food?

WHICH WOULD YOU CHOOSE?

Would you prefer to wear sticky shoes all day

very smelly clothes?

Would you prefer to be able to climb up tall buildings

shoot laser beams from your eyes?

Would you prefer to live in a tree house

in a house that sits on stilts over the sea?

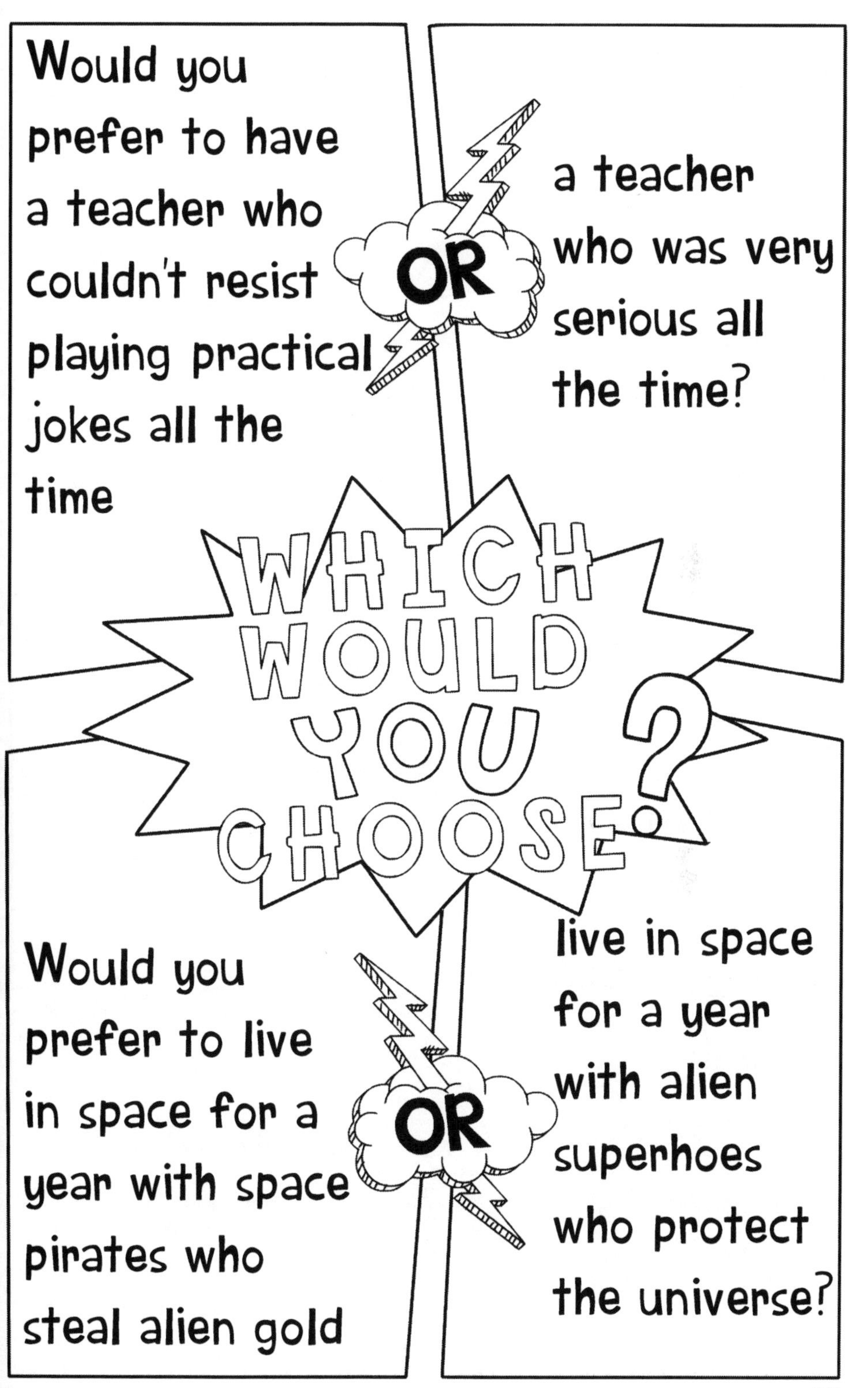
Would you prefer to have a teacher who couldn't resist playing practical jokes all the time
OR
a teacher who was very serious all the time?
WHICH WOULD YOU CHOOSE?
Would you prefer to live in space for a year with space pirates who steal alien gold
OR
live in space for a year with alien superhoes who protect the universe?

WHICH WOULD YOU CHOOSE?

Would you prefer to have an alien with two heads as your best friend

OR

a talking dragon?

Would you prefer to own a skateboard

rollerskates?

Would you prefer to be able to walk on your hands

do the splits?

Would you prefer to be a clumsy Ninja, who is always falling over
OR
or a flying superhero who often falls out of the sky?
WHICH WOULD YOU CHOOSE?
Would you prefer to be a tree that has magical powers but is rooted to the ground
OR
a tree that can walk and talk?

WHICH WOULD YOU CHOOSE?

Would you prefer to have sticky feet like a lizard

wings like a bird?

Would you prefer that tables had never been invented

chairs to sit on?

Would you prefer to live in the city

the countryside?

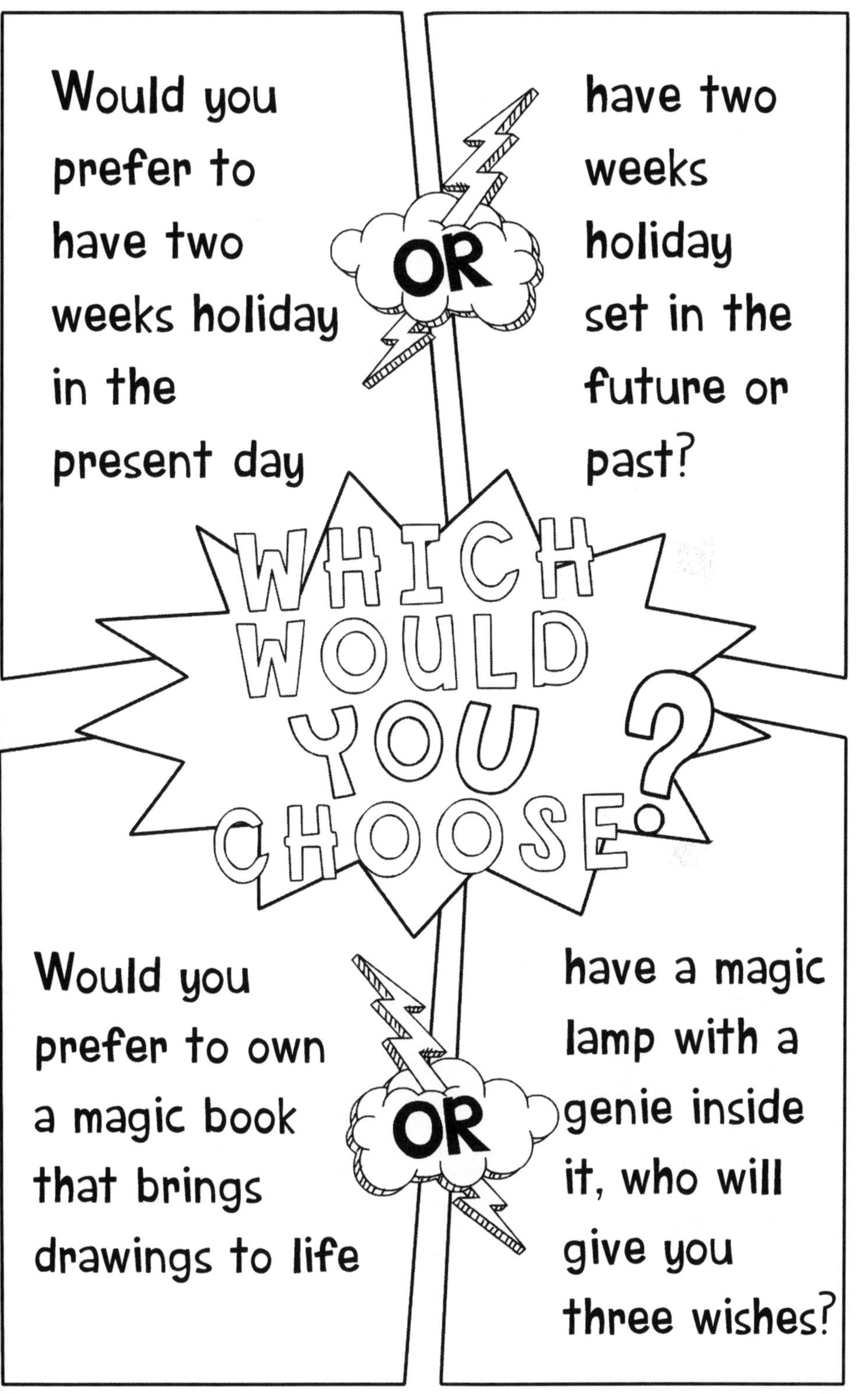
Would you prefer to have two weeks holiday in the present day
OR
have two weeks holiday set in the future or past?
WHICH WOULD YOU CHOOSE?
Would you prefer to own a magic book that brings drawings to life
OR
have a magic lamp with a genie inside it, who will give you three wishes?

WHICH WOULD YOU CHOOSE?

Would you prefer to have bananas for fingers

spaghetti for hair?

Would you prefer to ride on a giant phoenix

a dragon?

Would you prefer to be a successful detective

a successful super villain?

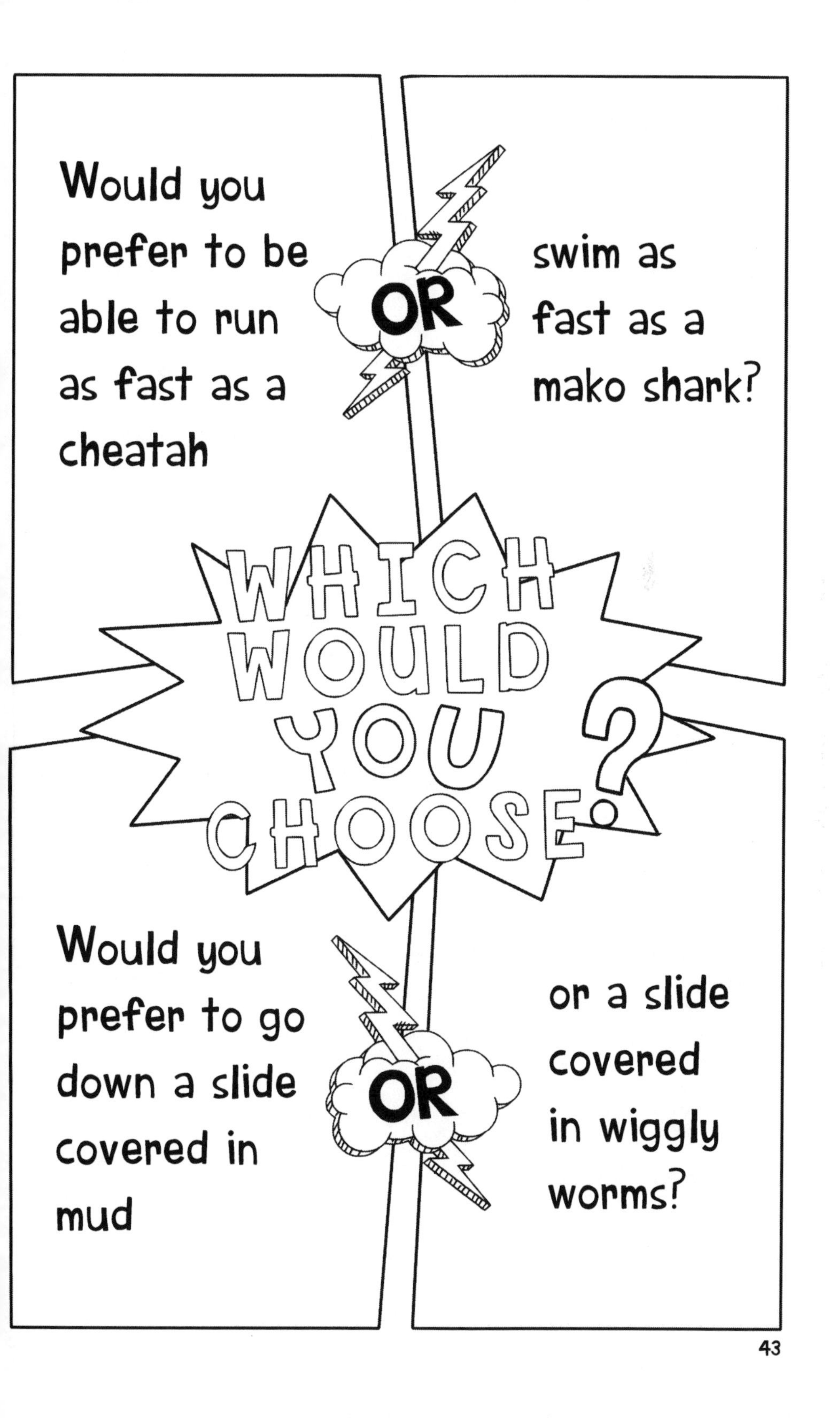
Would you prefer to be able to run as fast as a cheatah
OR
swim as fast as a mako shark?
WHICH WOULD YOU CHOOSE?
Would you prefer to go down a slide covered in mud
OR
or a slide covered in wiggly worms?

WHICH WOULD YOU CHOOSE?

Would you prefer to eat one small bulb of raw garlic

eat one whole large raw onion?

Would you prefer to be a unicorn with wings

a unicorn with no wings?

Would you prefer to wear flip flops

go barefoot?

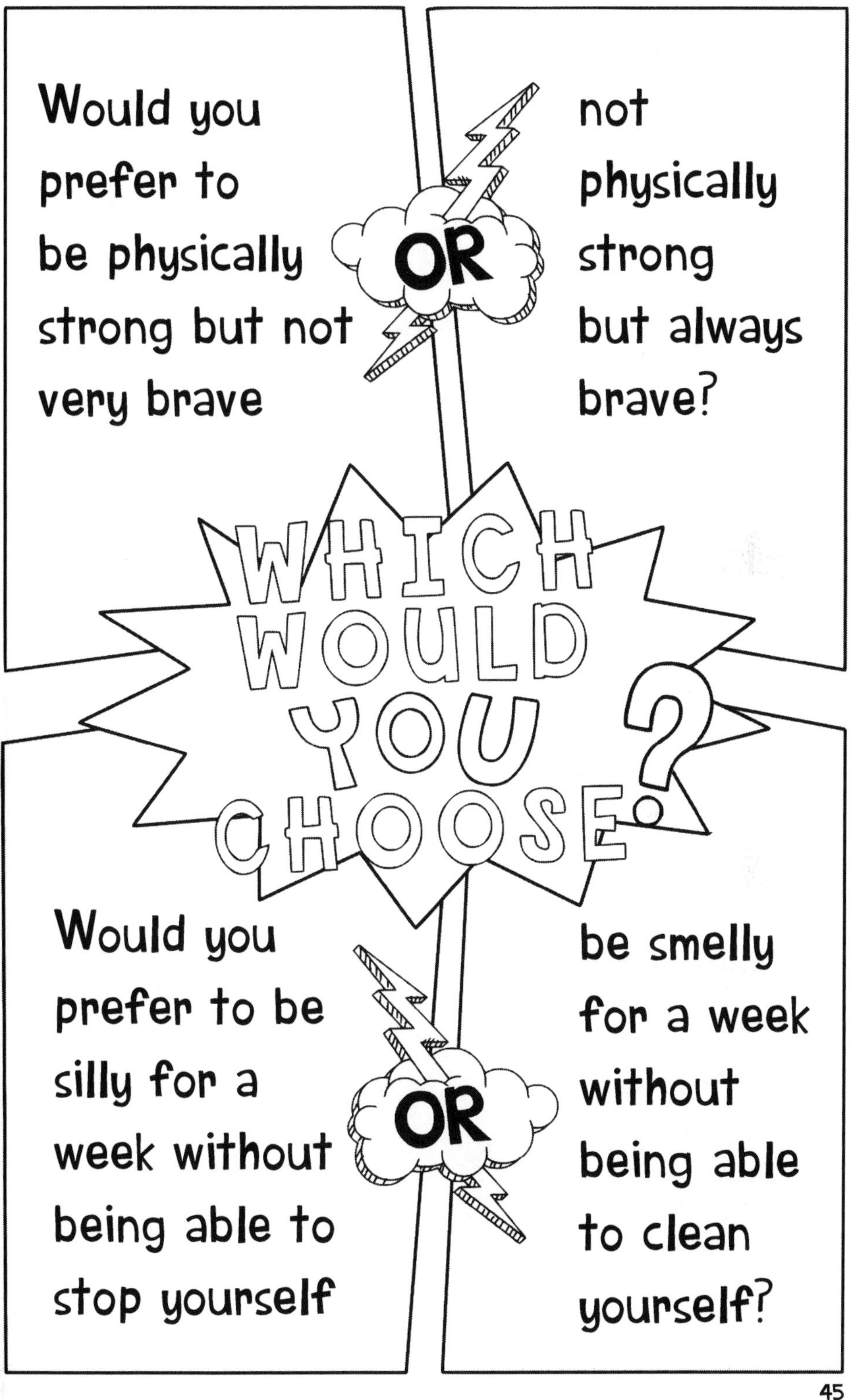
Would you prefer to be physically strong but not very brave
OR
not physically strong but always brave?
WHICH WOULD YOU CHOOSE?
Would you prefer to be silly for a week without being able to stop yourself
OR
be smelly for a week without being able to clean yourself?

WHICH WOULD YOU CHOOSE?

Would you prefer to be able to speed read

be able to solve any mathematical problem?

Would you prefer to have wings

have gills?

Would you prefer to be friends with a pirate

be friends with a mermaid?

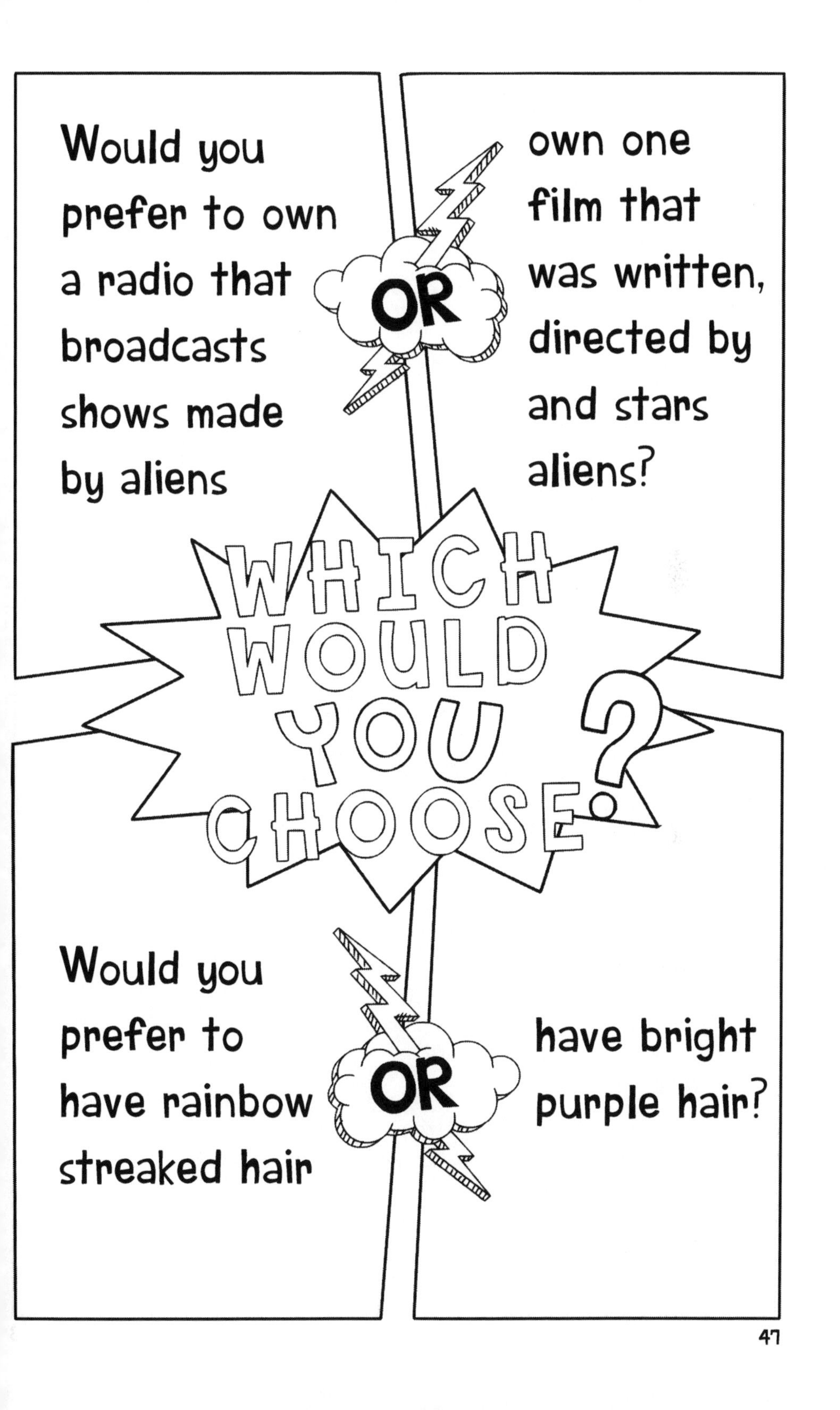
Would you prefer to own a radio that broadcasts shows made by aliens
OR
own one film that was written, directed by and stars aliens?
WHICH WOULD YOU CHOOSE?
Would you prefer to have rainbow streaked hair
OR
have bright purple hair?

WHICH WOULD YOU CHOOSE?

Would you prefer to have flowers growing out of your ears

have moss growing out of your nose?

Would you prefer to meet your favorite film star

meet your favorite author?

Would you prefer to go on holiday somewhere hot

somewhere cold?

Would you prefer to be able to read people's minds, but only if you hold their hands
OR
be able to read people's minds, but it's all of the time?
WHICH WOULD YOU CHOOSE?
Would you prefer to be able to work with animals in the jungle
OR
work with animals in the sea?

WHICH WOULD YOU CHOOSE?

Smell as bad as a wet dog for a week

smell like a skunk for a day?

Would you prefer that unicorns were real

mermaids were real?

Would you prefer to be 4 foot tall

be 7 foot tall?

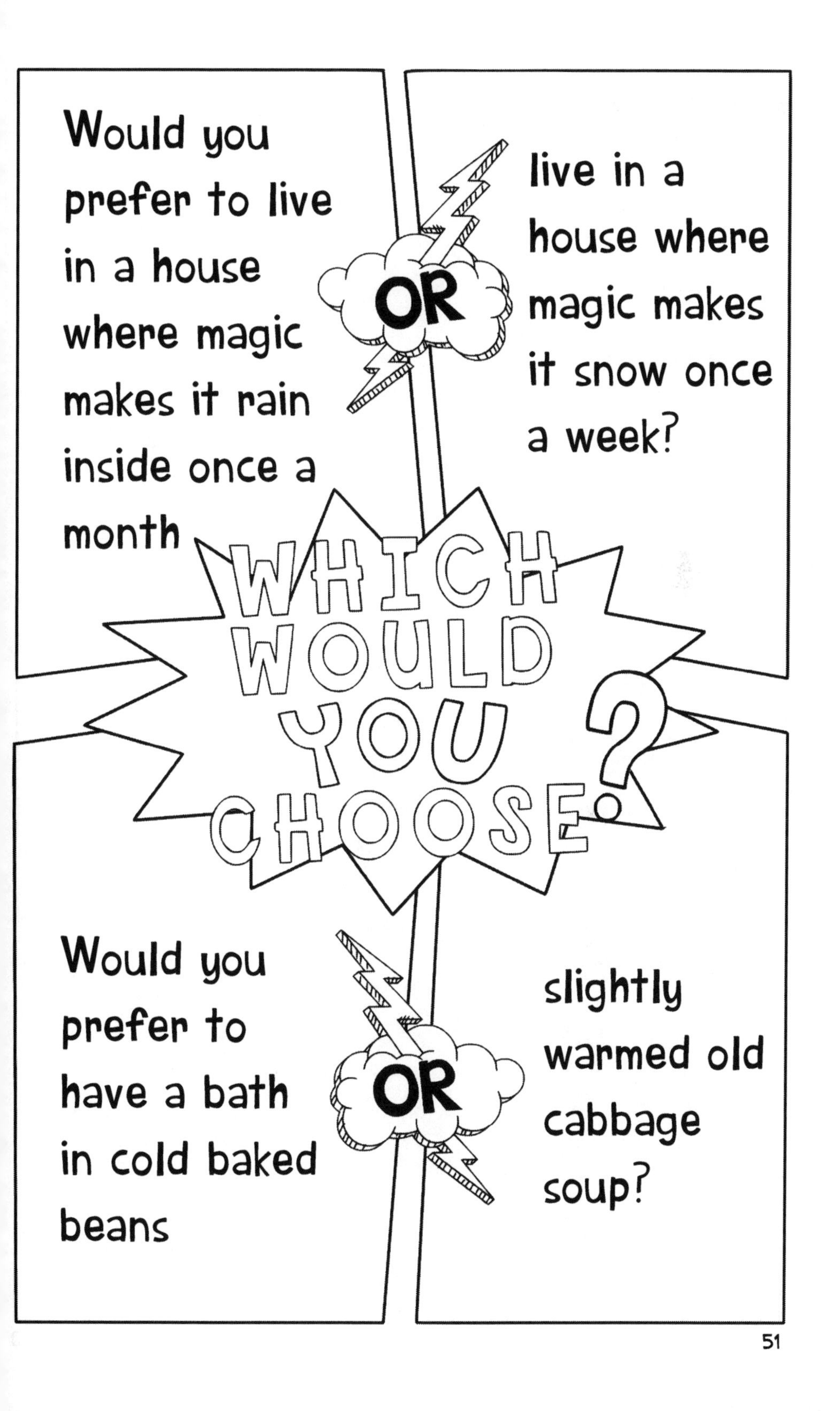
Would you prefer to live in a house where magic makes it rain inside once a month
OR
live in a house where magic makes it snow once a week?
WHICH WOULD YOU CHOOSE?
Would you prefer to have a bath in cold baked beans
OR
slightly warmed old cabbage soup?

WHICH WOULD YOU CHOOSE?

Would you prefer to sneeze fairies out of your nose

cough ant sized pirates out of your mouth?

Would you prefer to be a dolphin

a whale?

Would you prefer that watermelon didn't exist

pineapples?

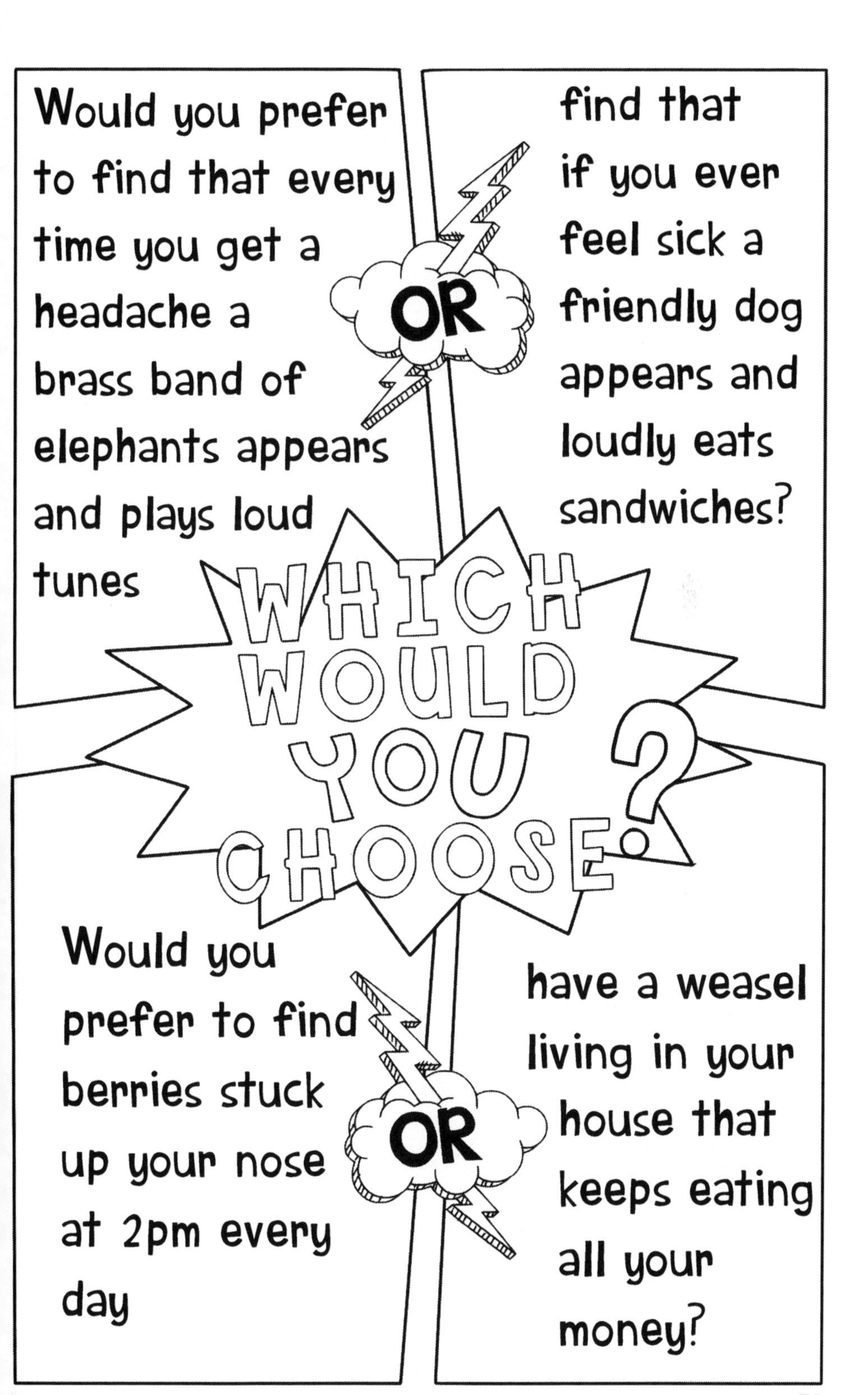
Would you prefer to find that every time you get a headache a brass band of elephants appears and plays loud tunes
OR
find that if you ever feel sick a friendly dog appears and loudly eats sandwiches?
WHICH WOULD YOU CHOOSE?
Would you prefer to find berries stuck up your nose at 2pm every day
OR
have a weasel living in your house that keeps eating all your money?

WHICH WOULD YOU CHOOSE?

Would you prefer to have a snow ball fight with your friend in winter

OR

play ball game with your friends in summer?

Would you prefer to walk across hot sand barefoot

OR

walk over ice barefoot?

Would you prefer to hitch a ride with a T-Rex

hitch a ride with a shark?

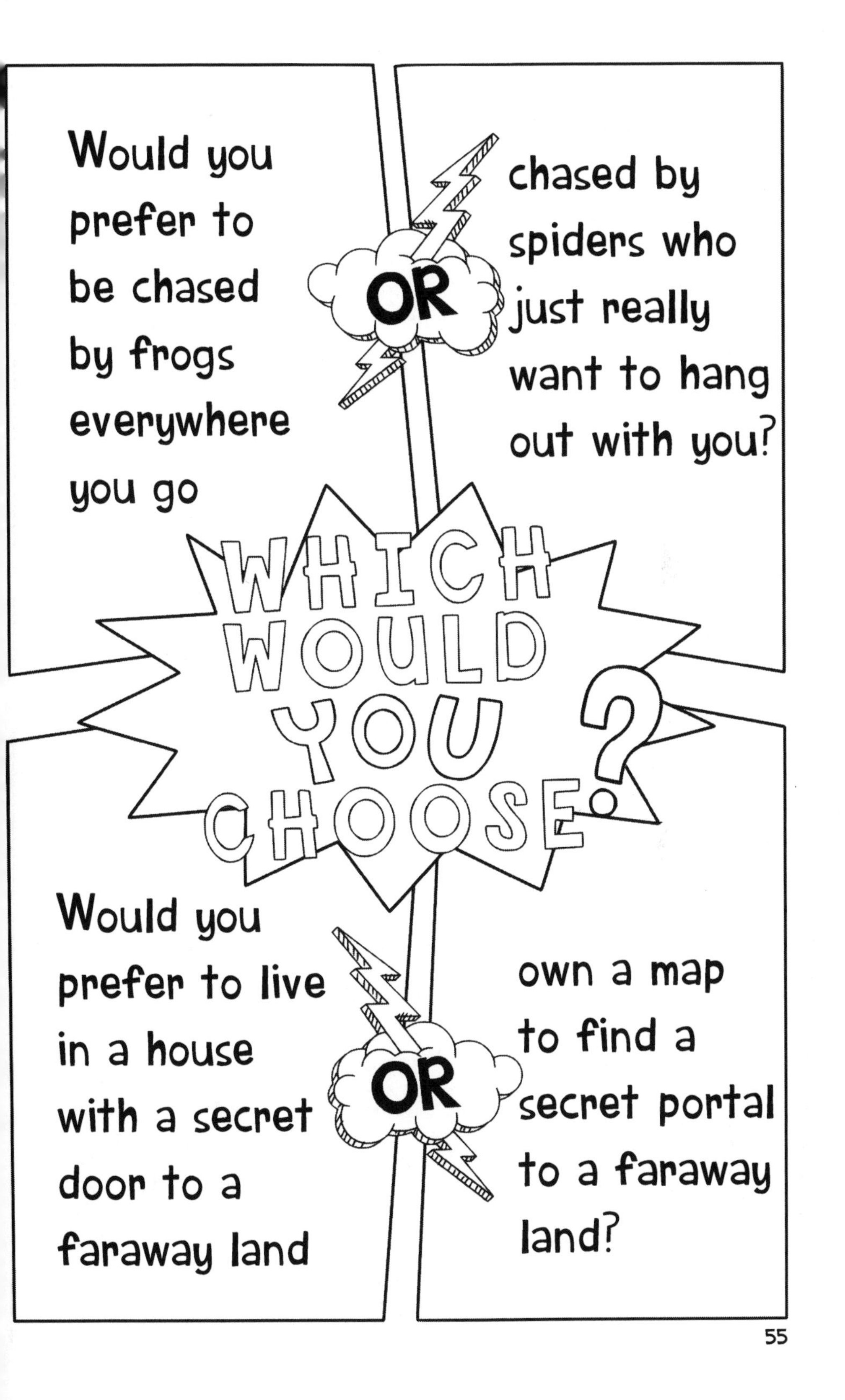
Would you prefer to be chased by frogs everywhere you go
OR
chased by spiders who just really want to hang out with you?
WHICH WOULD YOU CHOOSE?
Would you prefer to live in a house with a secret door to a faraway land
OR
own a map to find a secret portal to a faraway land?

WHICH WOULD YOU CHOOSE?

Would you prefer to go to school with beetles in your shoes

or with crickets in your hair?

Would you prefer to travel to school on a unicycle

or on a pogo stick?

Would you prefer to share a bedroom with a monkey

with a sloth?

Would you prefer to live in a house made of chocolate that melts on sunny days
OR
a house made of biscuits that goes soggy when it rains?
WHICH WOULD YOU CHOOSE?
Would you prefer to get to see a meteor shower at night
OR
a solar eclipse in the day?

WHICH WOULD YOU CHOOSE?

Would you prefer to see a rainbow

listen to a thunderstorm?

Would you prefer to sleep on a hard wooden floor

OR

sleep upside down from the ceiling like a bat?

Would you prefer to be able to predict the future

OR

be able to know what happened in the past?

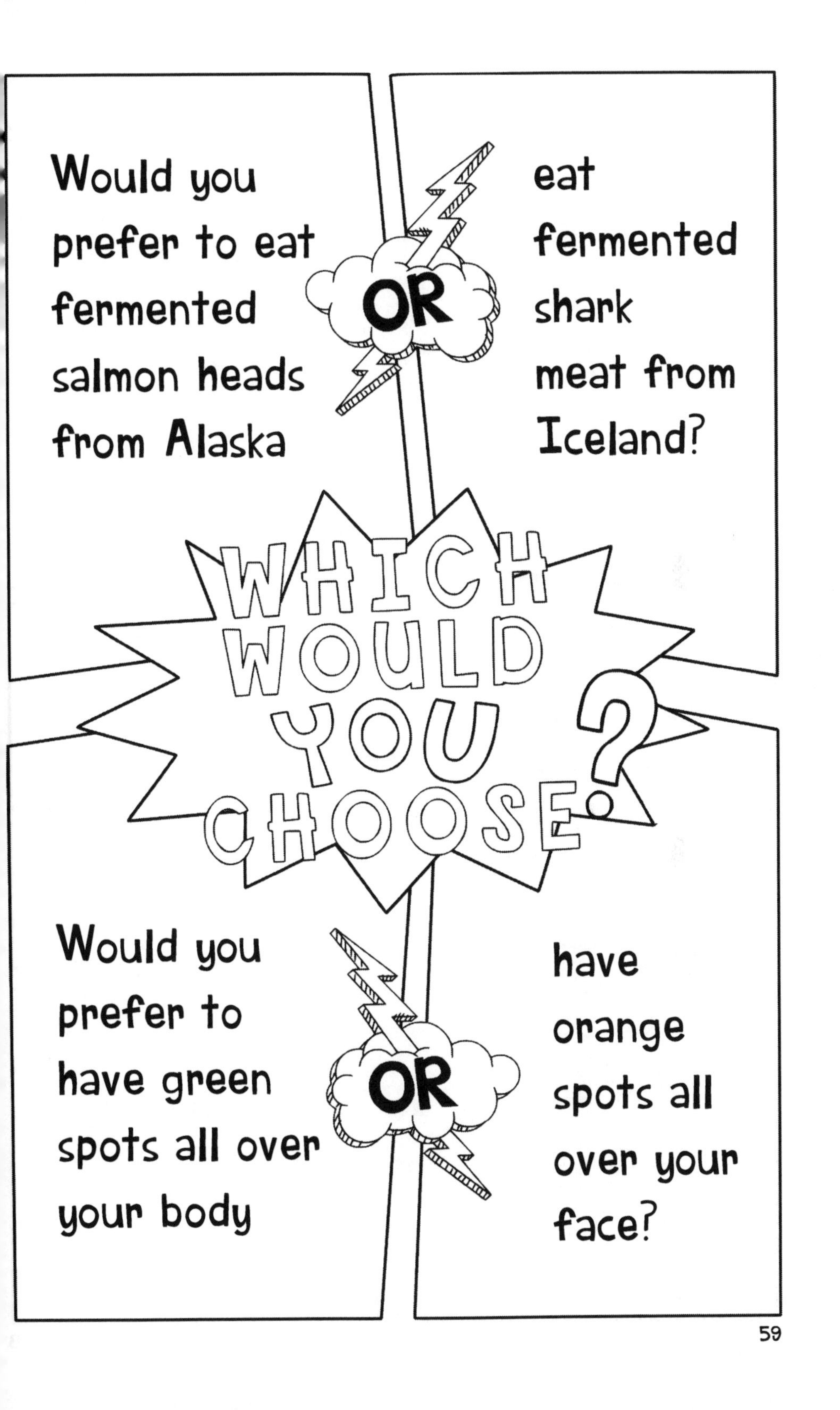
Would you prefer to eat fermented salmon heads from Alaska
OR
eat fermented shark meat from Iceland?
WHICH WOULD YOU CHOOSE?
Would you prefer to have green spots all over your body
OR
have orange spots all over your face?

WHICH WOULD YOU CHOOSE?

Would you prefer to know all the best jokes in the world

be able to sing all the best songs really well?

Would you prefer to wear clothes made from leaves

clothes made from straw?

Would you prefer to be the best singer in the world

or the best dancer?

Would you prefer to eat freeze dried space food every day at school for lunch?
OR
wear a spacesuit to go to school every day?
WHICH WOULD YOU CHOOSE?
Would you prefer to be 76 years old every other year that you live
OR
be 3 years old every other year that you live?

WHICH WOULD YOU CHOOSE?

Would you prefer to shrink to the size of a mouse

grow as tall as a house?

Would you prefer that strawberries did not exist

OR

oranges did not exist?

Would you prefer to go to the movies

go to a disco?

Would you prefer to learn to swim in a pool made of caramel but not be allowed to eat it
OR
have to sleep in a room made of candy but not be allowed to eat it?
WHICH WOULD YOU CHOOSE?
Would you prefer to have to say everything backwards first
OR
count to 100 first before you speak?

WHICH WOULD YOU CHOOSE?

Would you prefer to wear a creaky hat all day

squeaky shoes?

Would you prefer to be able to talk to farmyard animals

creatures from the ocean?

Would you prefer to feel too hot all day

too cold?

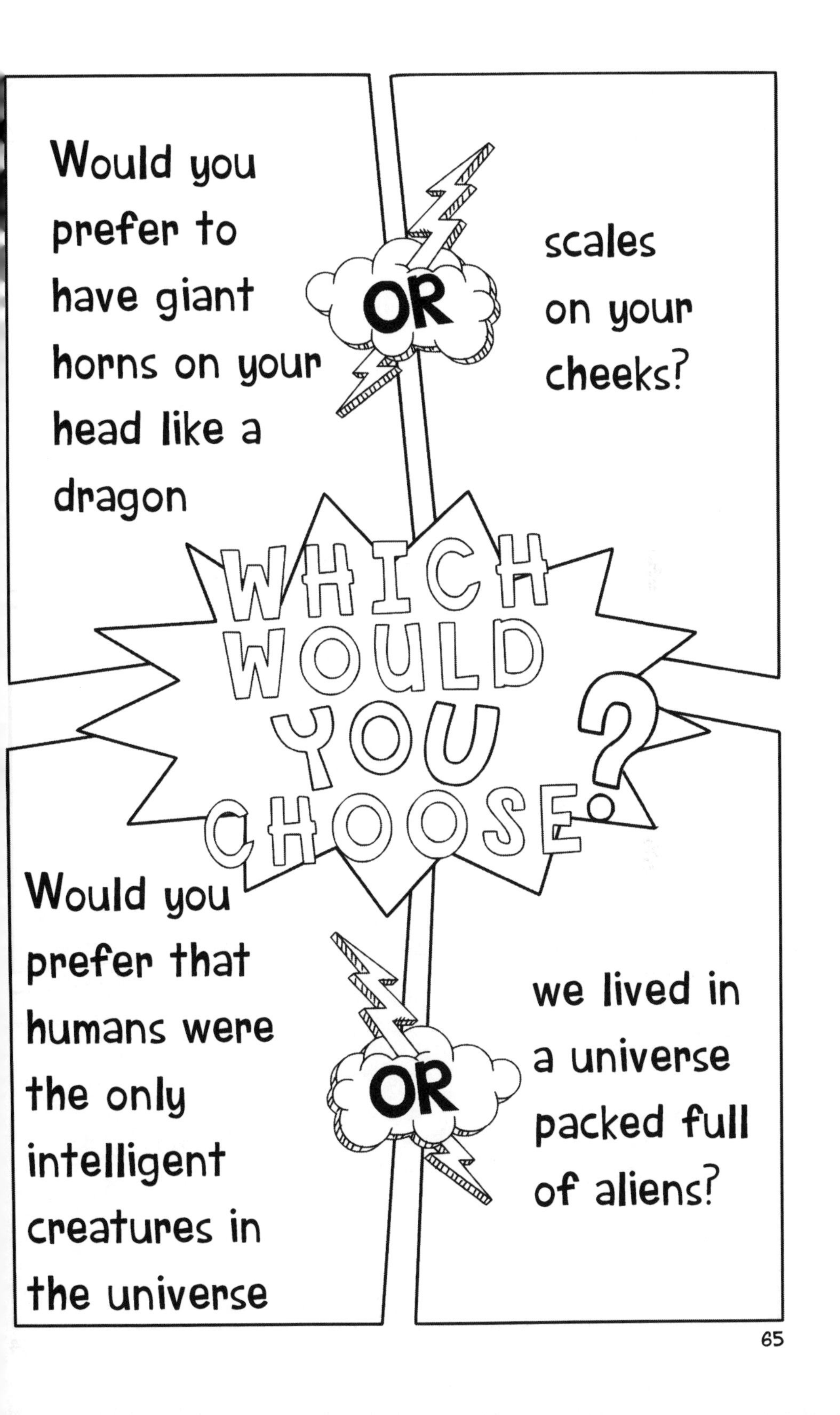
Would you prefer to have giant horns on your head like a dragon
OR
scales on your cheeks?
WHICH WOULD YOU CHOOSE?
Would you prefer that humans were the only intelligent creatures in the universe
OR
we lived in a universe packed full of aliens?

WHICH WOULD YOU CHOOSE?

Would you prefer to carry a goose everywhere you go

lead a lamb around behind you everywhere you go?

Would you prefer to eat raw vegetables

raw fish?

Would you prefer to play the piano

the guitar?

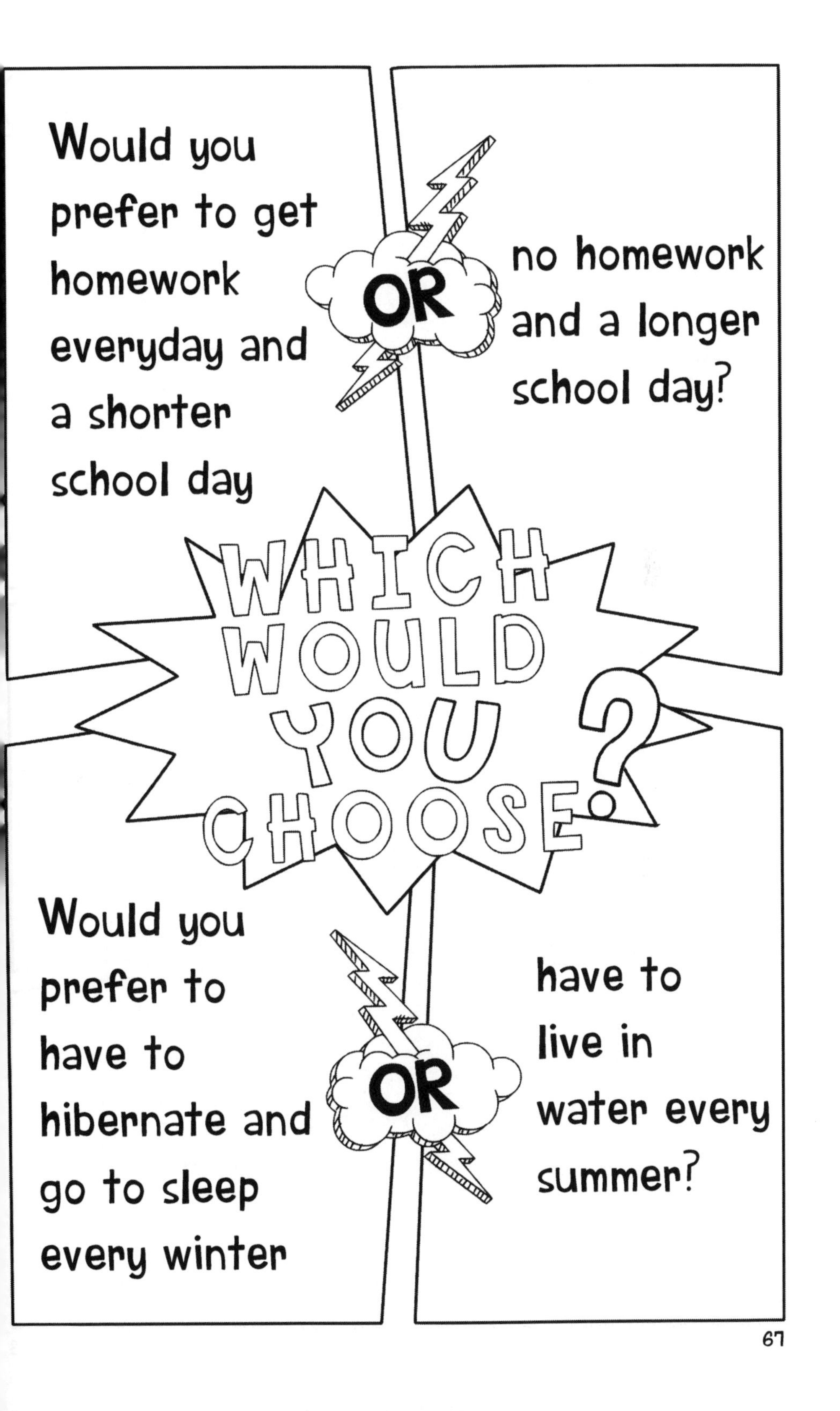
Would you prefer to get homework everyday and a shorter school day
OR
no homework and a longer school day?
WHICH WOULD YOU CHOOSE?
Would you prefer to have to hibernate and go to sleep every winter
OR
have to live in water every summer?

WHICH WOULD YOU CHOOSE?

Would you prefer to be accidentally stung by a friendly bee

OR

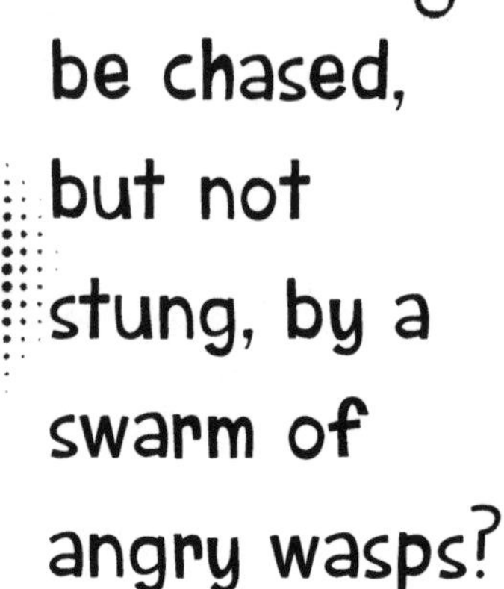

be chased, but not stung, by a swarm of angry wasps?

Would you prefer to eat Christmas pudding every day for a year

OR

eat spinach with every meal for a month?

Would you prefer to be a boxing kangaroo

OR

a sleepy koala?

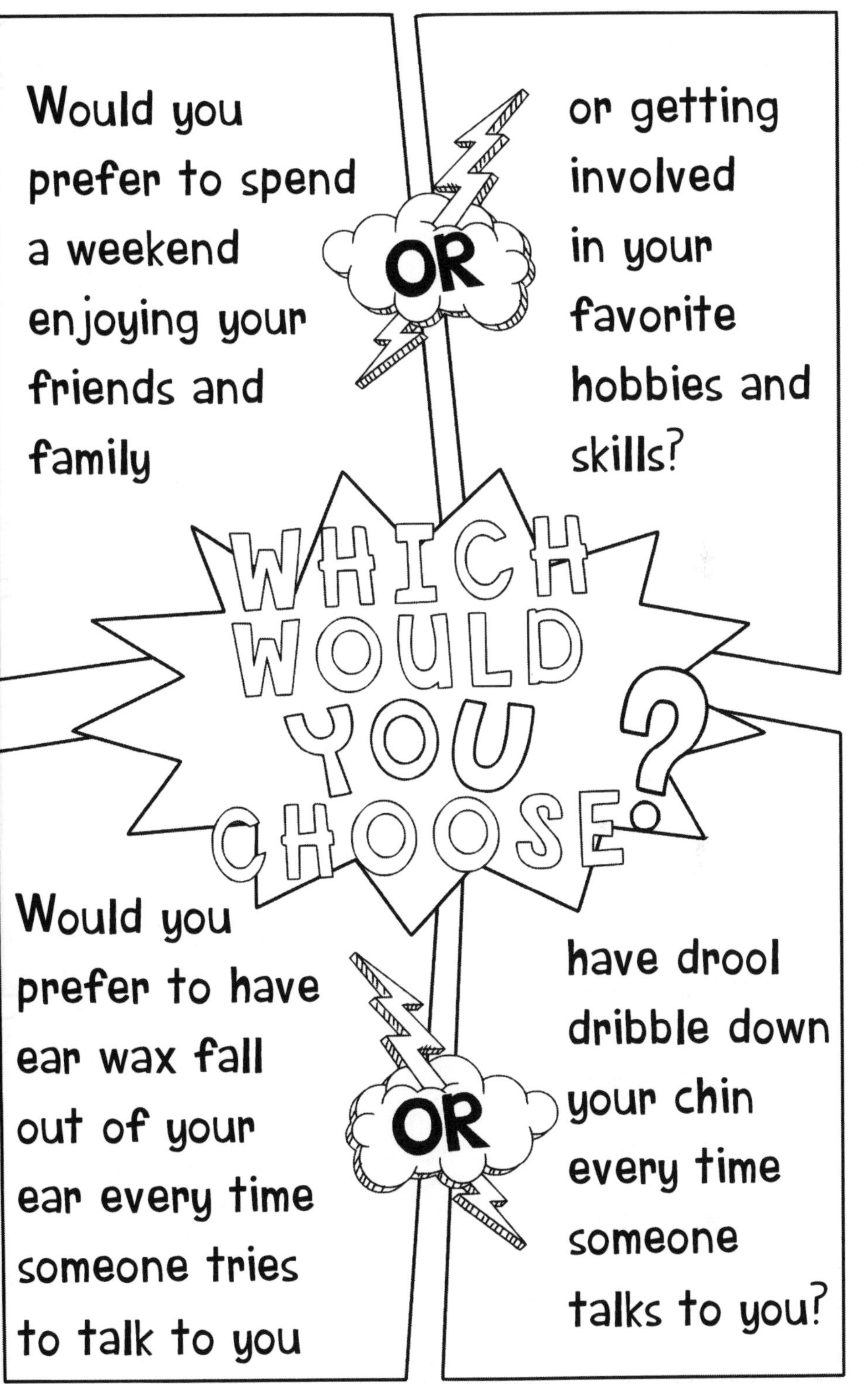
Would you prefer to spend a weekend enjoying your friends and family
OR
or getting involved in your favorite hobbies and skills?
WHICH WOULD YOU CHOOSE?
Would you prefer to have ear wax fall out of your ear every time someone tries to talk to you
OR
have drool dribble down your chin every time someone talks to you?

WHICH WOULD YOU CHOOSE?

Would you prefer to have to strut like a chicken all the time

waddle like a duck?

Would you prefer to blow a trumpet when you walk into a room

shake a tambourine before you speak?

Would you prefer to hand feed a goose

hand feed a goat?

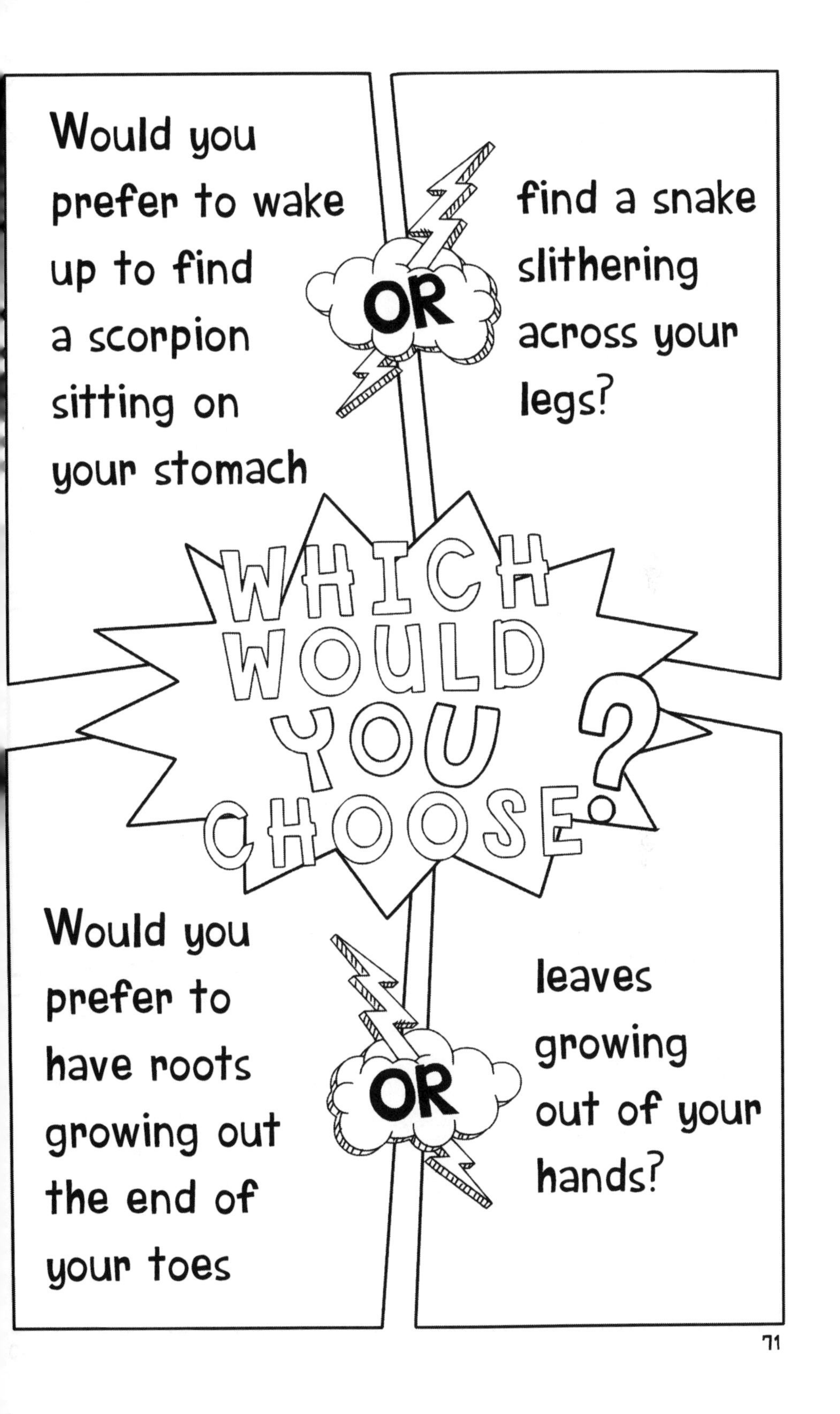
Would you prefer to wake up to find a scorpion sitting on your stomach
OR
find a snake slithering across your legs?
WHICH WOULD YOU CHOOSE?
Would you prefer to have roots growing out the end of your toes
OR
leaves growing out of your hands?

WHICH WOULD YOU CHOOSE?

Would you prefer to have a teacher who turns out to be a witch

OR

or a teacher who turns out to be an elf?

Would you prefer to age forwards

age backwards?

Would you prefer to eat worms

eat snails?

Would you prefer to be able to take a stroll on the moon
OR
a vacation on Mars?
WHICH WOULD YOU CHOOSE?
Would you prefer to have your teeth cleaned by a scorpion
OR
have your hair cut by a crocodile?

WHICH WOULD YOU CHOOSE?

Would you prefer that cars were never invented

toys were never invented?

Would you prefer to get stuck in a bathroom

get stuck in an elevator?

Would you prefer to have legs as long as an adult body

arms that go all the way down to the floor?

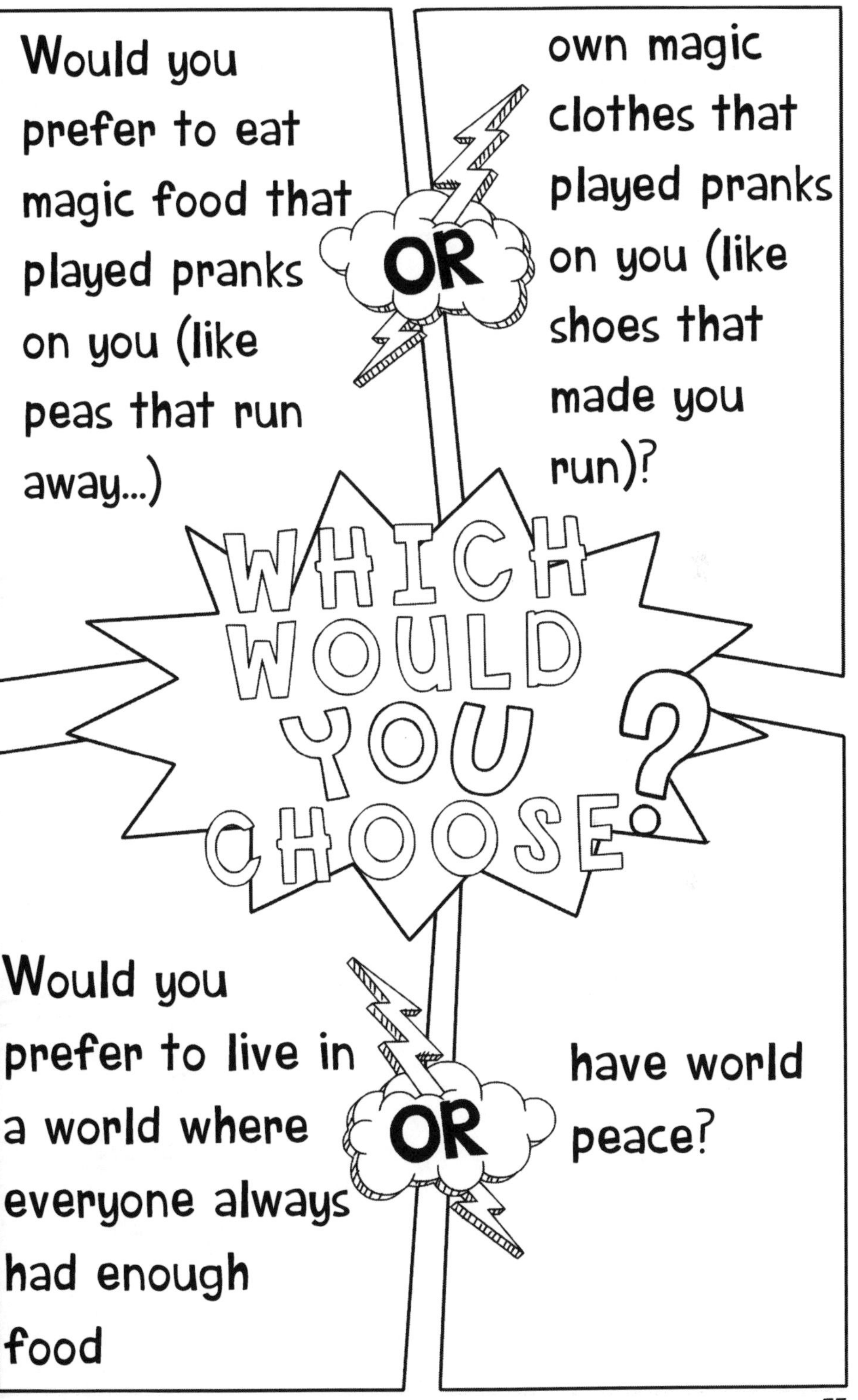
Would you prefer to eat magic food that played pranks on you (like peas that run away...)
OR
own magic clothes that played pranks on you (like shoes that made you run)?
WHICH WOULD YOU CHOOSE?
Would you prefer to live in a world where everyone always had enough food
OR
have world peace?

WHICH WOULD YOU CHOOSE?

Would you prefer to learn superhero skills at school

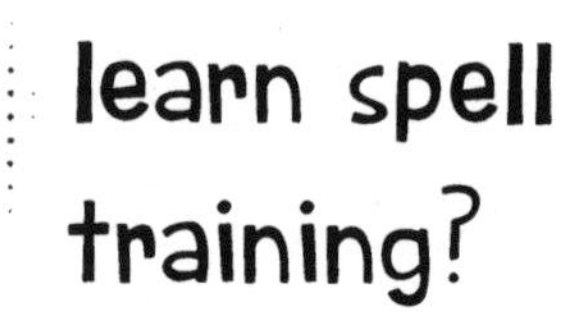

OR

learn spell training?

Would you prefer to have a bird live on your head

have a weasel live up your sleeve?

Would you prefer to be able to turn invisible

be able to travel to other dimensions?

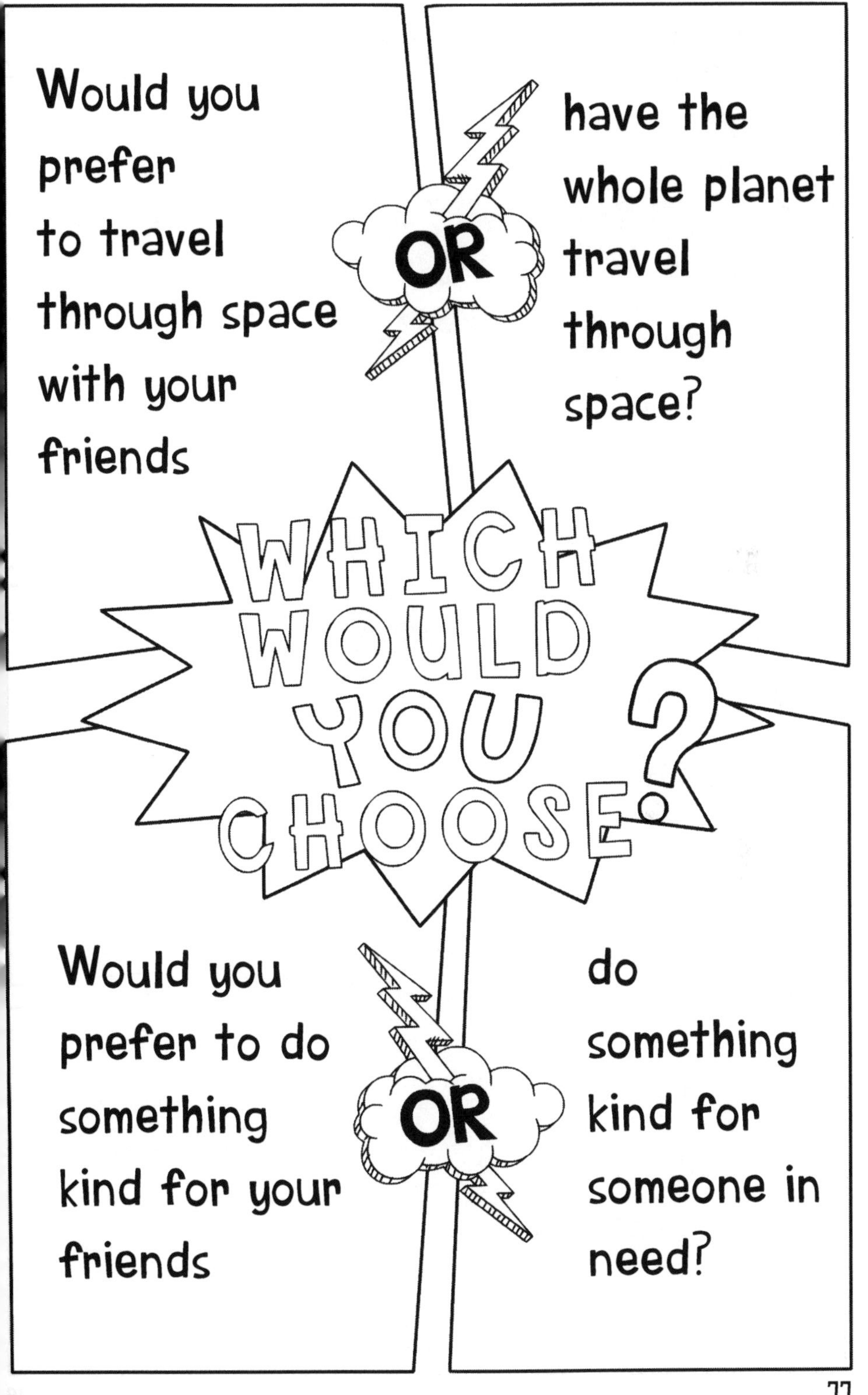
Would you prefer to travel through space with your friends
OR
have the whole planet travel through space?
WHICH WOULD YOU CHOOSE?
Would you prefer to do something kind for your friends
OR
do something kind for someone in need?

WHICH WOULD YOU CHOOSE?

Would you prefer to find an eel in your bath

find frog spawn in your drink?

Would you prefer to have a sleepover with a mischievious yak

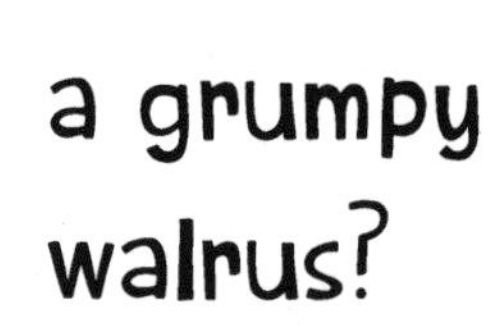

a grumpy walrus?

Would you prefer to be a mermaid

a robot?

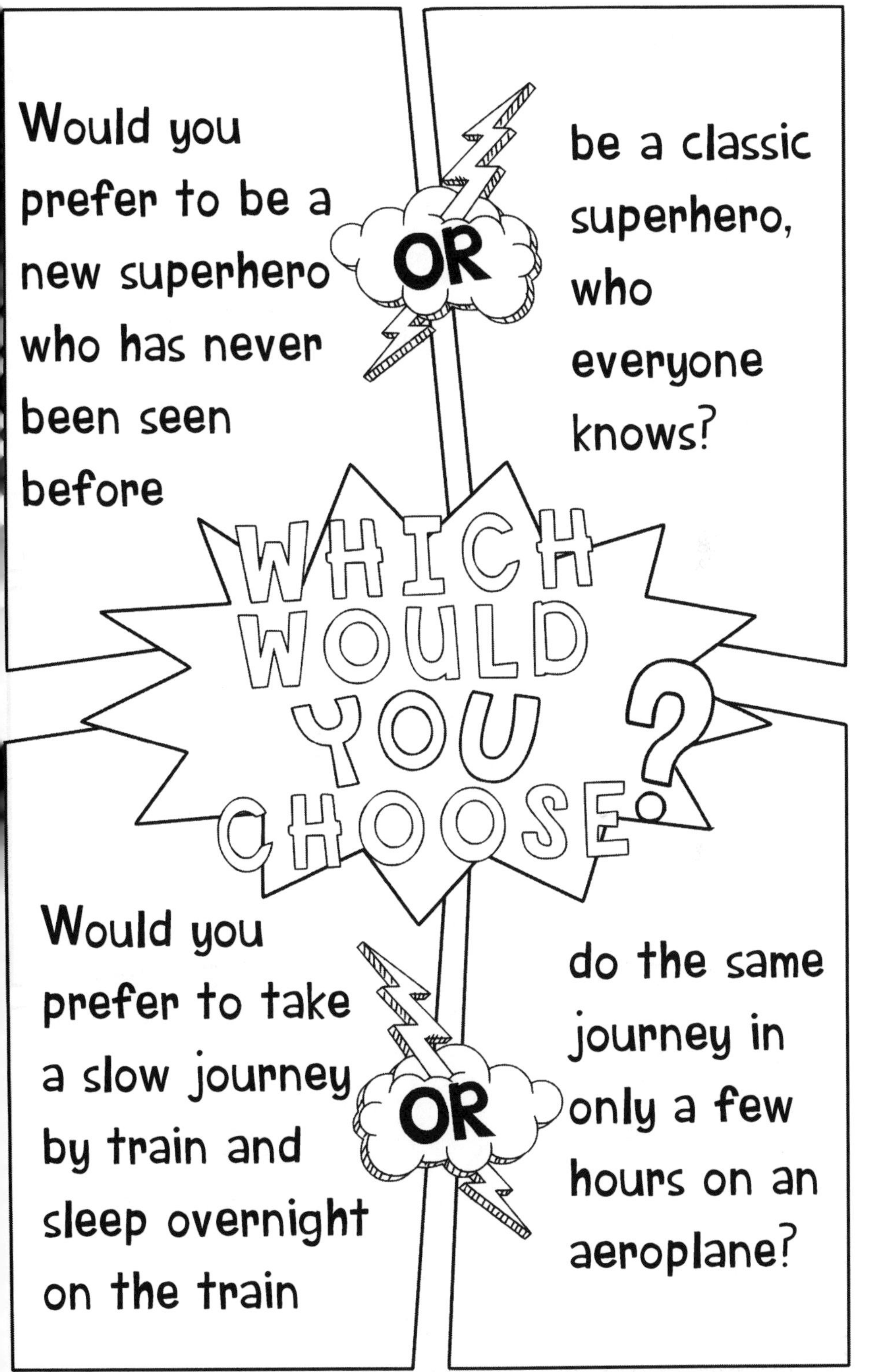
Would you prefer to be a new superhero who has never been seen before
OR
be a classic superhero, who everyone knows?
WHICH WOULD YOU CHOOSE?
Would you prefer to take a slow journey by train and sleep overnight on the train
OR
do the same journey in only a few hours on an aeroplane?

WHICH WOULD YOU CHOOSE?

Would you prefer to blow up like a balloon and be able to float

OR

stretch like a rubber band and be able to leap tall buildings?

Would you prefer to swim with dolphins

see a narwhal whilst standing on a boat?

Would you prefer to live in a house full of pet birds

a house full of pet cats?

Would you prefer to have only water to drink for one month (no choice of other drinks)
OR
have only healthy food as the choice of food for one month (no treats)?
WHICH WOULD YOU CHOOSE?
Would you prefer to have a bright red 'mohican' hair style
OR
have long green hair like a witch?

WHICH WOULD YOU CHOOSE?

Would you prefer to get stuck in a maze with a talking frog

OR

a singing unicorn?

Would you prefer to have to wriggle your way into a room

OR

beat box on your way out?

Would you prefer a big red pimple on the end of your nose

OR

a very sore pimple on your bottom?

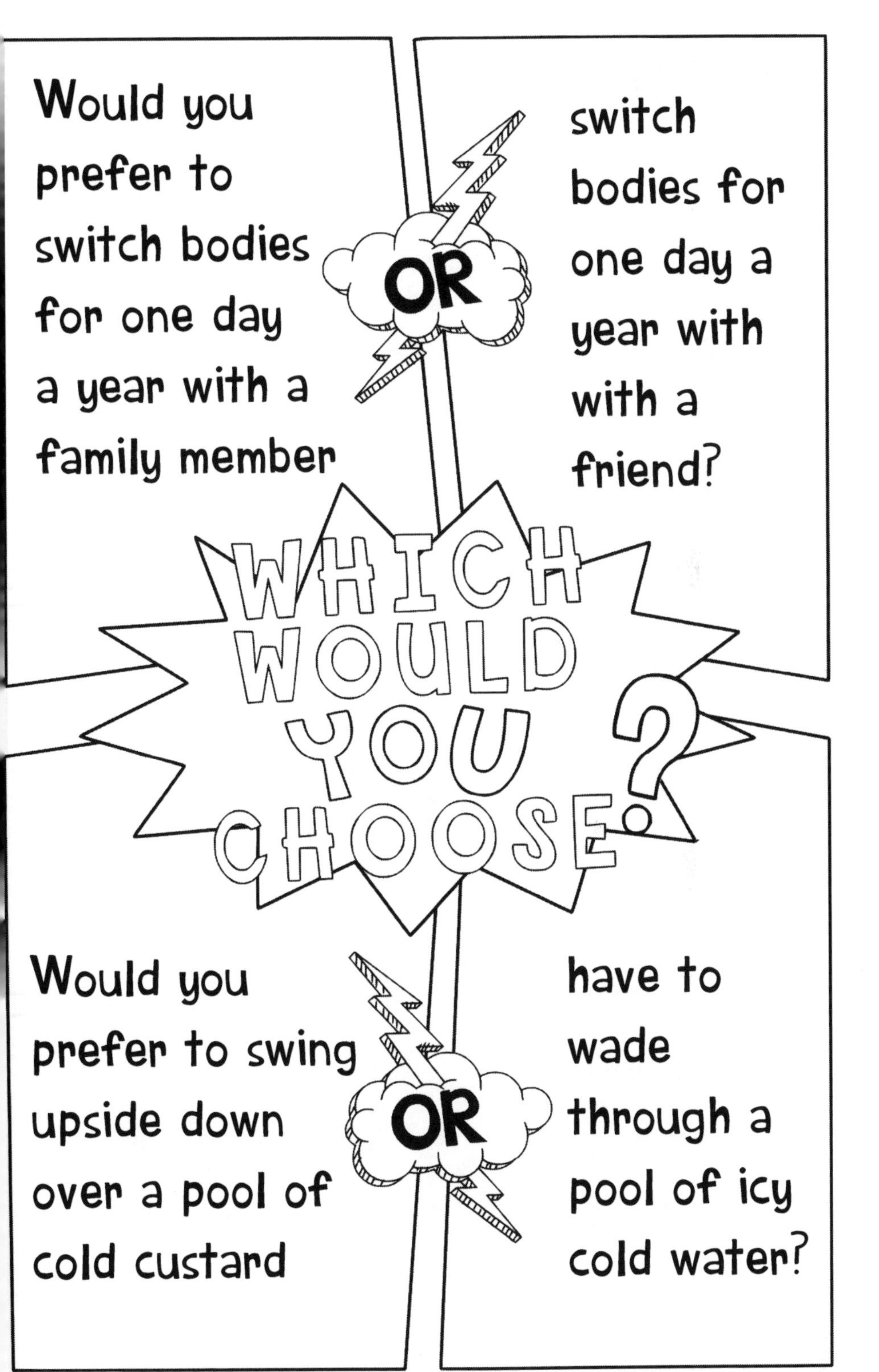
Would you prefer to switch bodies for one day a year with a family member
OR
switch bodies for one day a year with with a friend?
WHICH WOULD YOU CHOOSE?
Would you prefer to swing upside down over a pool of cold custard
OR
have to wade through a pool of icy cold water?

WHICH WOULD YOU CHOOSE?

Would you prefer to walk everywhere outside on stilts

OR

only ever be able to walk backwards?

Would you prefer to go to the zoo

OR

a water park?

Would you prefer to have whiskers like a cat

or the tail of a dog?

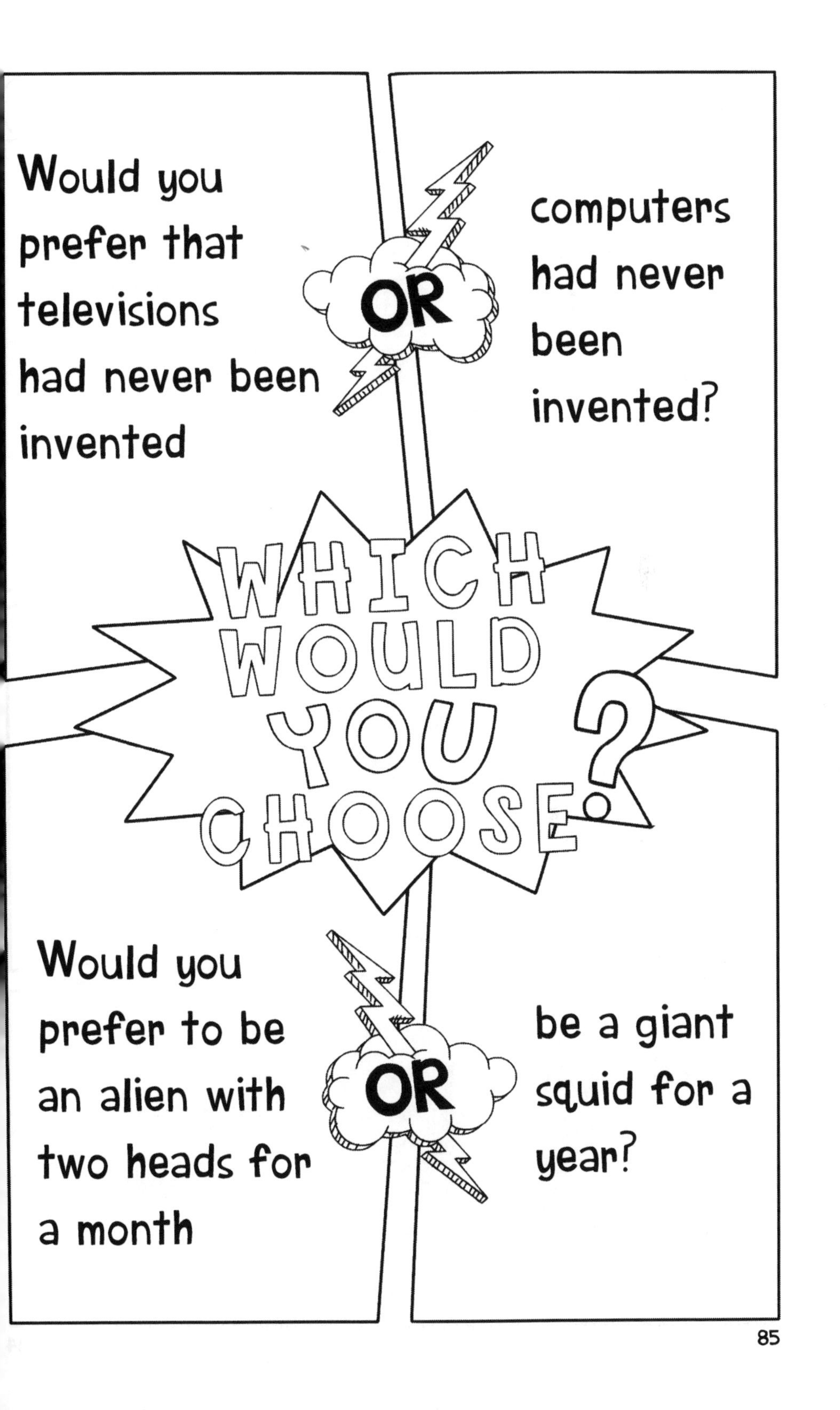
Would you prefer that televisions had never been invented
OR
computers had never been invented?
WHICH WOULD YOU CHOOSE?
Would you prefer to be an alien with two heads for a month
OR
be a giant squid for a year?

WHICH WOULD YOU CHOOSE?

Would you prefer to be a Christmas Elf

be the Easter bunny?

Would you prefer to build a snowman that comes to life

meet Santa?

Would you prefer to be a year older

a year younger?

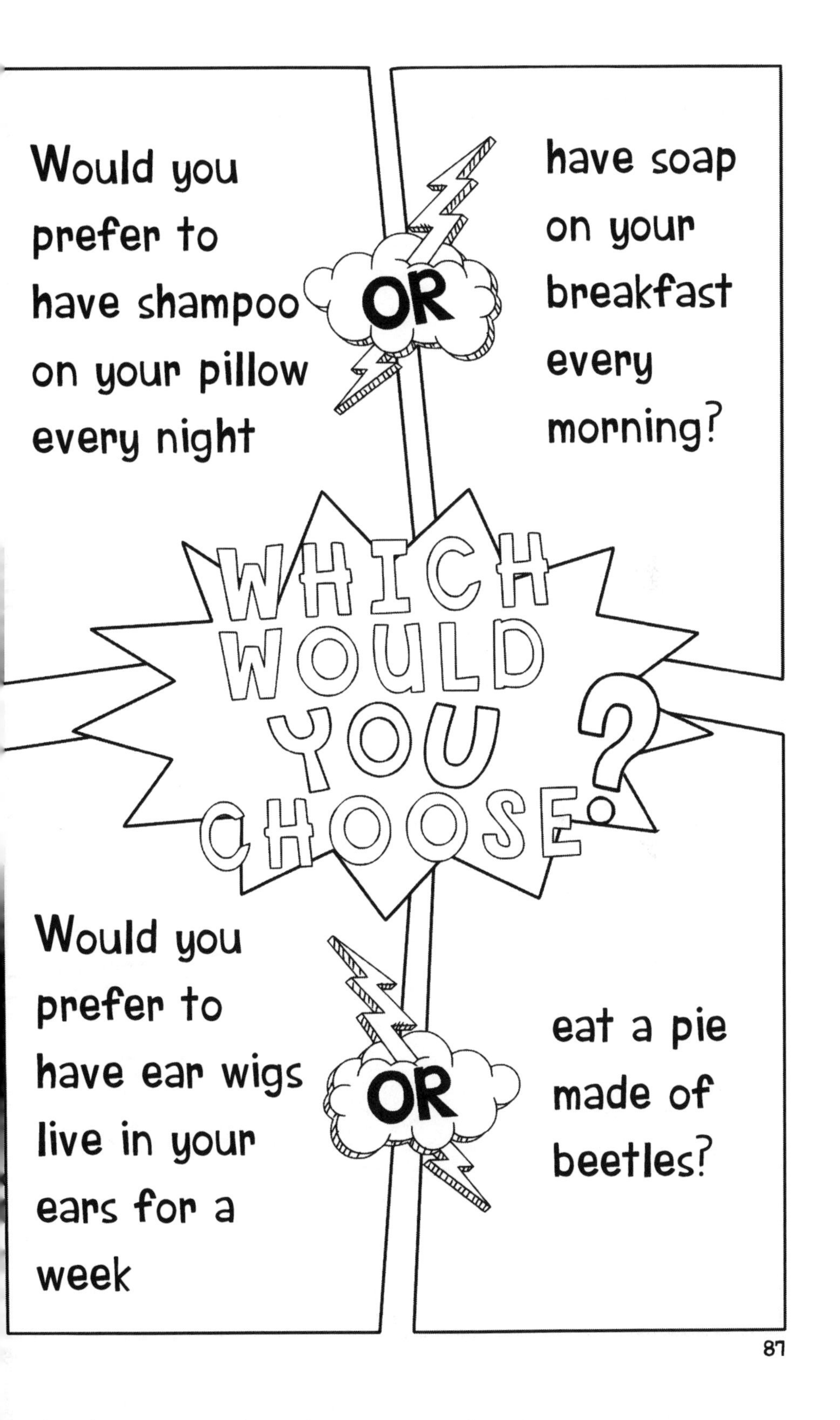
Would you prefer to have shampoo on your pillow every night
OR
have soap on your breakfast every morning?
WHICH WOULD YOU CHOOSE?
Would you prefer to have ear wigs live in your ears for a week
OR
eat a pie made of beetles?

WHICH WOULD YOU CHOOSE?

Would you prefer to wear an outfit made of orange peel

wear an outfit made of banana skins?

Would you prefer to be able to sneeze gold

cry pearls from your eyes?

Would you prefer to be able to speak 8 different languages

understand how to build any machine you want to?

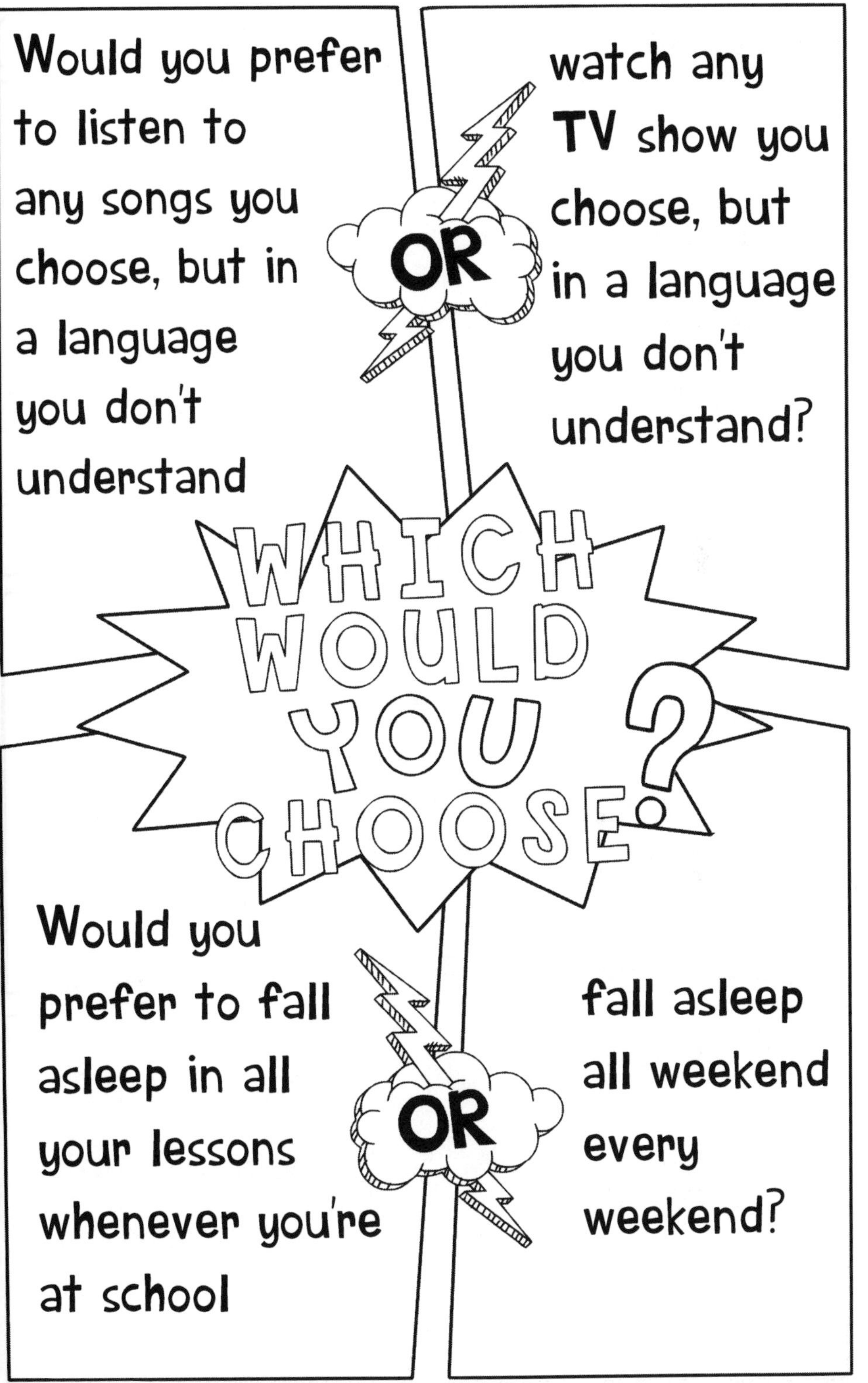
Would you prefer to listen to any songs you choose, but in a language you don't understand
OR
watch any TV show you choose, but in a language you don't understand?
WHICH WOULD YOU CHOOSE?
Would you prefer to fall asleep in all your lessons whenever you're at school
OR
fall asleep all weekend every weekend?

WHICH WOULD YOU CHOOSE?

Would you prefer to have yodel practise every morning at school

learn an opera song by heart?

Would you prefer to be able to bounce really high

OR

be able to roll down hills really fast?

Would you prefer to be able to turn invisible any time you like

OR

be able to fly, but only one day a week?

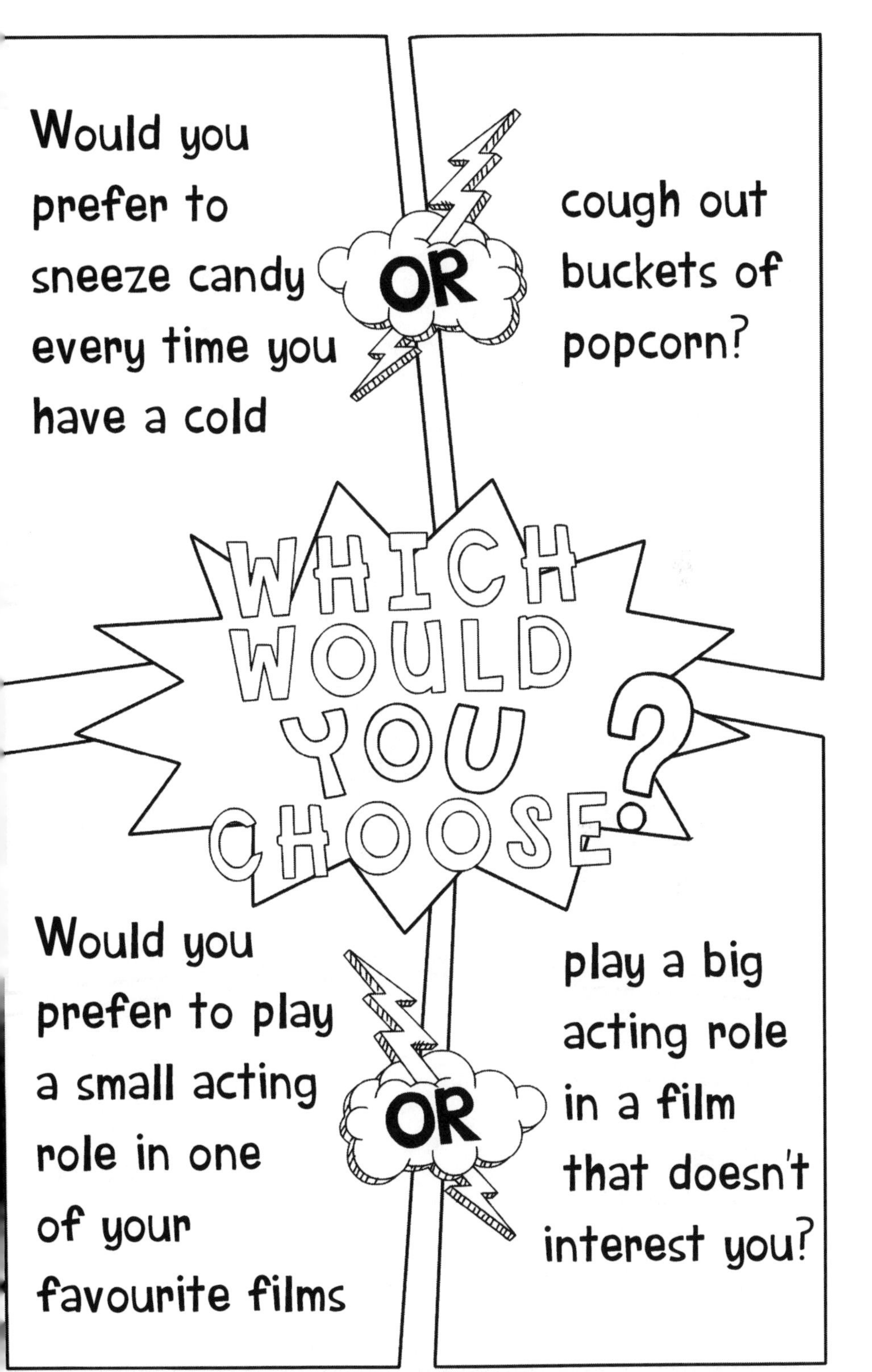
Would you prefer to sneeze candy every time you have a cold
OR
cough out buckets of popcorn?
WHICH WOULD YOU CHOOSE?
Would you prefer to play a small acting role in one of your favourite films
OR
play a big acting role in a film that doesn't interest you?

WHICH WOULD YOU CHOOSE?

Would you prefer to have to sing everything you want to say

OR

have to write it down?

Would you prefer to invent a way to teleport

a time machine?

Would you prefer to live in a teepee

a lighthouse?

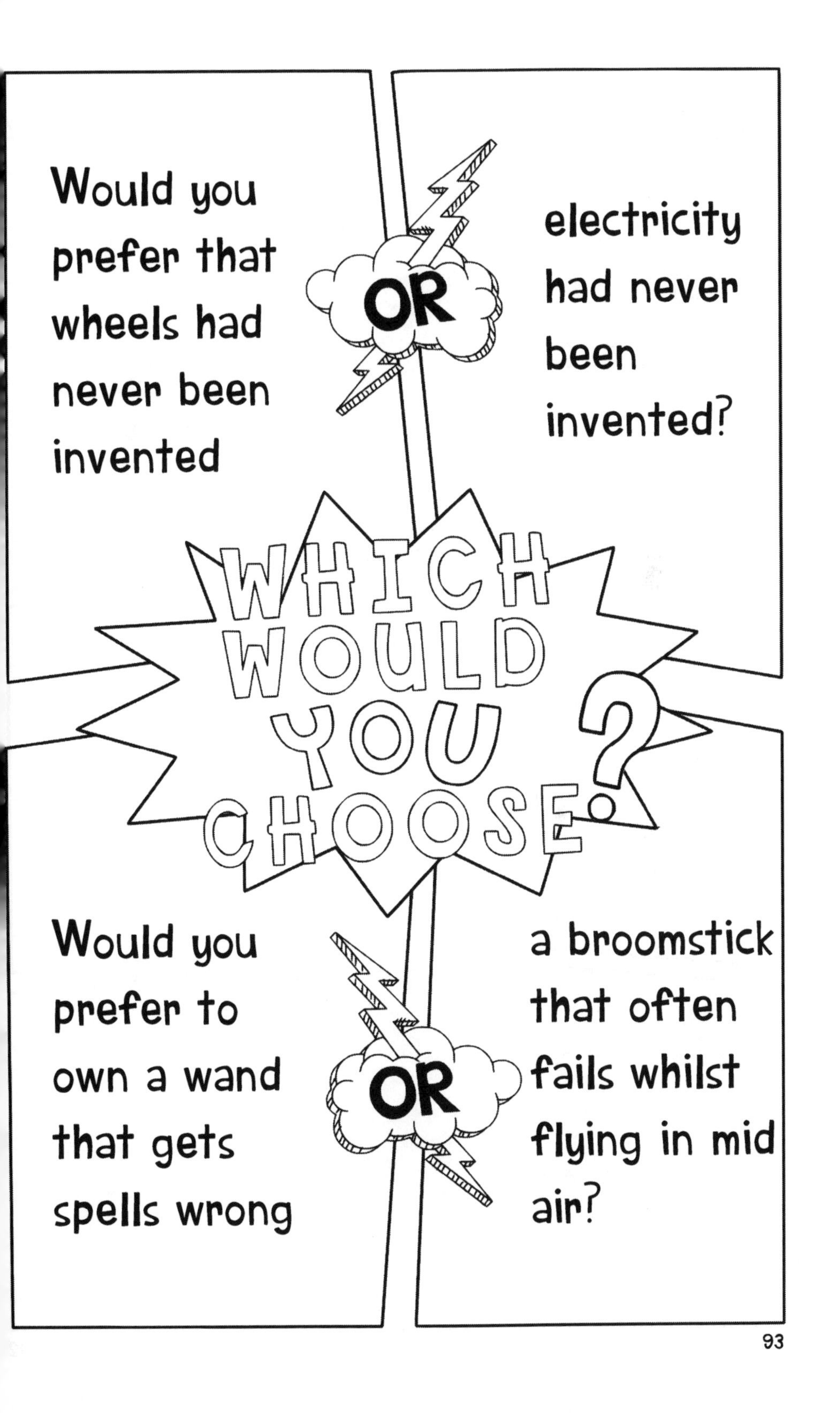
Would you prefer that wheels had never been invented
OR
electricity had never been invented?
WHICH WOULD YOU CHOOSE?
Would you prefer to own a wand that gets spells wrong
OR
a broomstick that often fails whilst flying in mid air?

WHICH WOULD YOU CHOOSE?

Would you prefer to makes mistakes and learn from them

OR

never make mistakes and not learn very much?

Would you prefer to be able to perform perfect ballet

perfect break dancing?

Would you prefer to eat a diet of only raw food

a vegan diet?

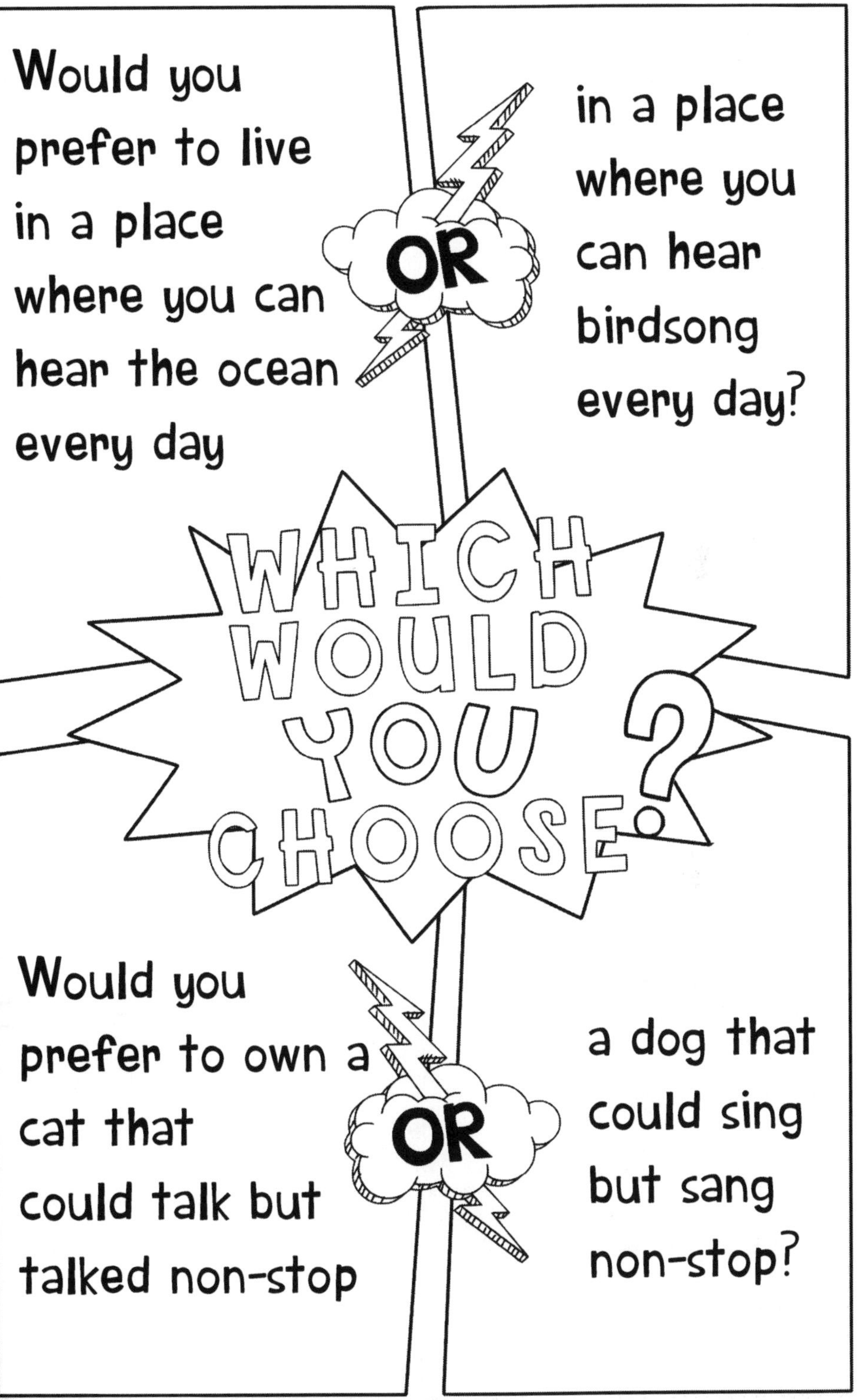
Would you prefer to live in a place where you can hear the ocean every day
OR
in a place where you can hear birdsong every day?
WHICH WOULD YOU CHOOSE?
Would you prefer to own a cat that could talk but talked non-stop
OR
a dog that could sing but sang non-stop?

WHICH WOULD YOU CHOOSE?

Would you prefer to have no sunlight all the time

have not enough sleep all the time?

Would you prefer to have your friends turn into snails

your family turn into moths?

Would you prefer to live in a house but have no clothes

have clothes but no house to live in?

Would you prefer to own a dog that eats things out of the bin
OR
or a cat that drinks out of the toilet?
WHICH WOULD YOU CHOOSE?
Would you prefer to be sneezed on by a gigantic alien squid from Mars
OR
fall into the slime trail of a humungous slug monster from Uranus?

WHICH WOULD YOU CHOOSE?

Would you prefer to have an elephant sit on your car

OR

a skunk taking a nap in your bed?

Would you prefer to invent a new sport

invent a new type of cuisine?

Would you prefer to wear only pink clothes

only blue clothes?

Would you prefer to be an architect
OR
be a dancer?
WHICH WOULD YOU CHOOSE?
Would you prefer to have no sense of taste
OR
have no sense of smell?

WHICH WOULD YOU CHOOSE?

Would you prefer that there was no bread in the world

OR

no pasta?

Would you prefer to save the planet from certain doom singlehandedly

OR

as part of a team?

Would you prefer to have ants inside your pants

OR

up your nose?

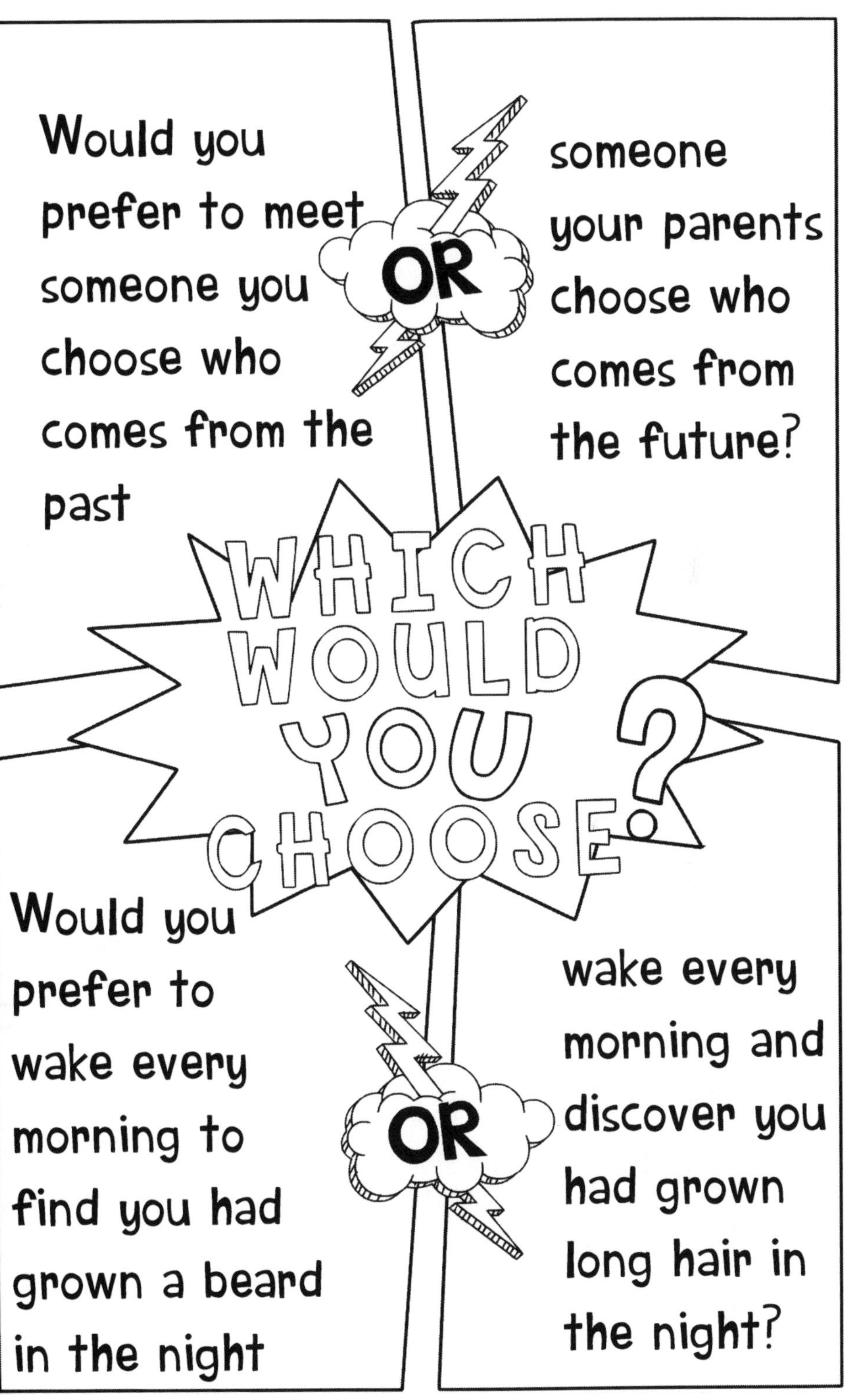
Would you prefer to meet someone you choose who comes from the past
OR
someone your parents choose who comes from the future?
WHICH WOULD YOU CHOOSE?
Would you prefer to wake every morning to find you had grown a beard in the night
OR
wake every morning and discover you had grown long hair in the night?

WHICH WOULD YOU CHOOSE?

Would you prefer that the planet was made of marshmallows

OR

or jelly?

Would you prefer to be kind

right?

Would you prefer to be able to stop time

freeze individual people for short periods of time?

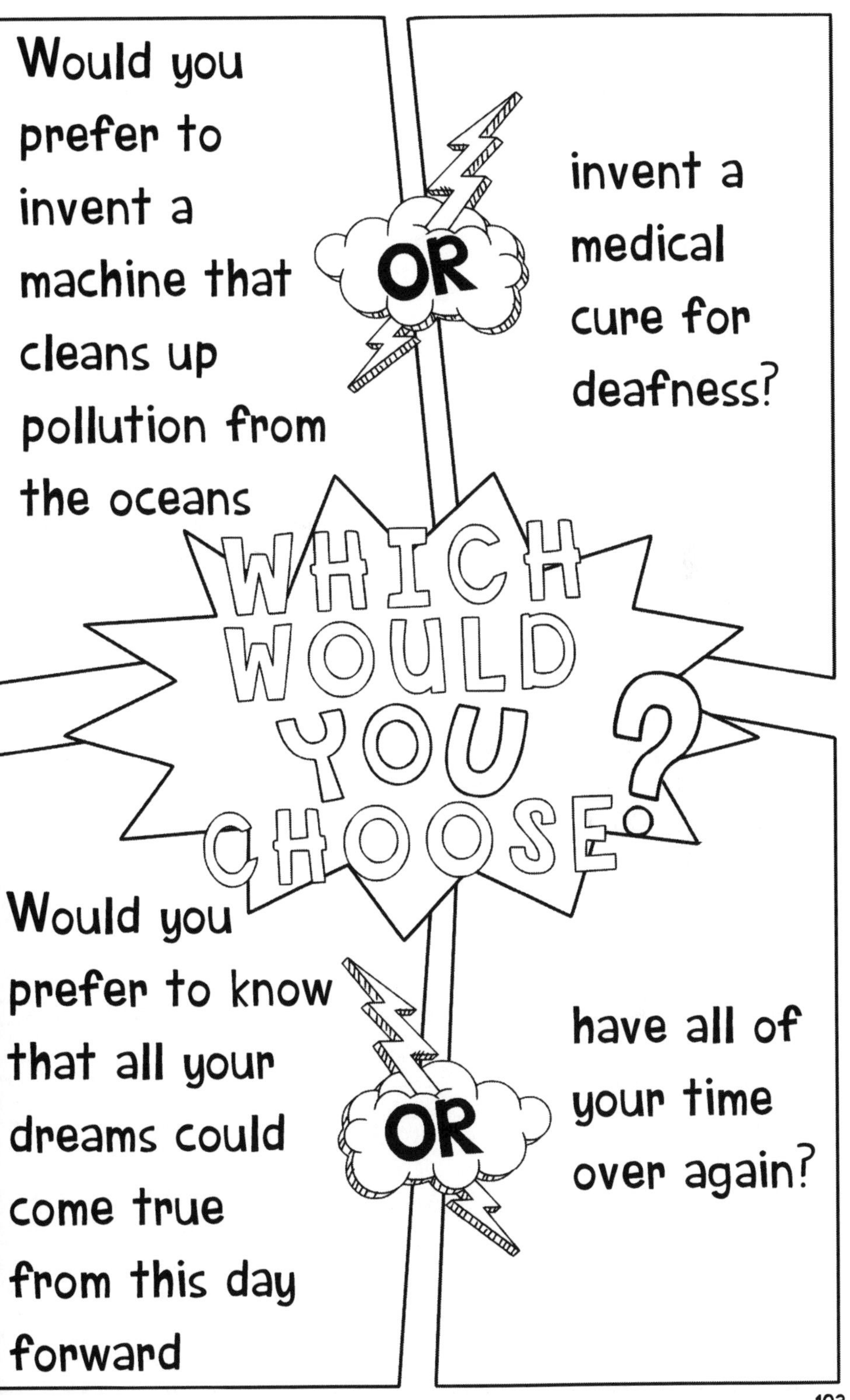
Would you prefer to invent a machine that cleans up pollution from the oceans
OR
invent a medical cure for deafness?
WHICH WOULD YOU CHOOSE?
Would you prefer to know that all your dreams could come true from this day forward
OR
have all of your time over again?

Before you go...

What? Wait? You answered every single question in the book? Awesome.

Why not try this tip for the silliest way to make the questions go further?

The person asking the question reads the first half of the scenario out and then chooses the second half from a different question ending on the same page or double page.

Can you find new questions that still make sense as a sentence?

Thanks for reading...

If you enjoyed the book please consider leaving an honest review on Amazon. It lets other people know what's good about the book.

Thank-you!

Made in the USA
Middletown, DE
28 February 2020